TEN LIVES DECLARING HUMAN RIGHTS

From

Bartolome de Las Casas

to

Martin Luther King Jr.

* * *

by
Michael Curtotti

Foreword by Chris Sidoti

ALDILA PRESS

Copyright © 2020, 2023 Michael Curtotti

All rights reserved. No part of this book may be reproduced, or stored in a retrieval system, or transmitted in any form or by any means, electronic, mechanical, photocopying, recording, or otherwise, without express written permission of the author.

Published by Aldila Press Pty Ltd, Ngunnawal Country/Canberra, 2023.

3rd paperback edition

ISBN 978-0-6458446-3-4

Cover Image

Adapted from Adam Jones from Kelowna, BC, Canada - 18th-Century Slave Shackles from Tamale, Northern Ghana - International Slavery Museum - Liverpool - England, CC BY-SA 2.0, https://commons.wikimedia.org/w/index.php?curid=64196413

Dedication

To those
who have given us human rights;
and to those to come

Table of Contents

Foreword .... *i*
Preface .... *v*
Introduction .... *ix*
CHAPTER ONE Bartolome de Las Casas *1*
CHAPTER TWO Thomas Clarkson *13*
CHAPTER THREE Lucretia Mott *19*
CHAPTER FOUR Tahirih *27*
CHAPTER FIVE Frederick Douglass *37*
CHAPTER SIX Alain Locke *49*
CHAPTER SEVEN Primo Levi *59*
CHAPTER EIGHT Eleanor Roosevelt *67*
CHAPTER NINE Martin Luther King Jr. *75*
CHAPTER TEN Albie Sachs *111*
CHAPTER ELEVEN Epilogue *117*
Bibliography *119*
About the Author *125*
By the Same Writer *127*

Foreword

Human rights concern people. Human beings. Human rights arise from human experience – the actual, real life experiences of real people, with their joys and hopes, their fears and anxieties. Human rights are revealed and affirmed by people – first and foremost, those who suffer and struggle and then also the activists and the academics and the statespersons. Human rights are from people, for people.

We human beings seem to like to complicate things. We have built an enormous body of law, nationally and internationally, to define human rights and then the lawyers among us, and I include myself among those lawyers, set about interpreting and applying that law and arguing about that law. It all becomes so complicated. But, in fact, human rights are very simple. Ask anyone – a child, a parent, a worker, someone who is hungry or homeless or illiterate or unemployed, a person imprisoned or tortured for religious or political beliefs or on account of ethnicity or culture or gender or sexual orientation – what is fair and what is unfair and that person knows. People are able to reflect on experience and answer the question, with telling insight and profound meaning. They know what it means to be human and what a human being needs to live a fully human life.

Human rights are very simple. They are simply an attempt to define in legal terms what it means to be human and to describe in legal terms what a human being requires to live a fully human life. It's not complicated, is it? That definition and that description come from human experiences. They come above all from the experiences of war and persecution and suffering and from the leadership and commitment of inspired individuals and mass movements of people who have been determined that all human beings have a right to be treated with dignity and respect as equals.

Michael Curtotti has made a significant contribution to human rights as a lawyer, writer and academic. His work has not been ivory tower work, even though it has had a rigorously academic and intellectual basis. It has been work to make human rights known to and understood by us all so that we all take up the work of human rights.

This little book is part of Michael's life's work. It presents human rights through the lives of ten individuals who have made major contributions to the development of human rights, even though many of them would have never heard the term. The ten are very different from each other. They have lived over the past 500 years in very different parts of the planet. All but one (Albie Sachs being the exception) is dead. All but one (Eleanor Roosevelt being the exception) did not live lives of privilege. Many of them experienced serious human rights violations. Four of them suffered gravely for their human rights work – Tahirih and Martin Luther King Jnr were murdered, Primo Levi was driven to suicide, Albie Sachs was seriously injured by an assassination attempt. Frederick Douglass had been a slave and Alain Locke was an African American who lived under segregation. Lucretia Mott experienced discrimination as a woman, as did Eleanor Roosevelt in many respects. All of them witnessed the gravest forms of human rights violation. For all of them their human rights work was firmly grounded in their life experiences. Human rights come from human experience.

In telling these stories, even briefly, this book brings human rights 'close to home', where universal human rights begin, as Eleanor Roosevelt put it. Michael Curtotti has again done us all a great service in this.

I write this foreword with a hope: that those who read it will see and understand human rights in all their simplicity and that they will commit themselves anew to walking with millions of others to the mountaintop, as Martin Luther King Jnr did, and then on to the promised land of justice, love and peace that he saw on the other side.

Chris Sidoti

Preface

This book, although short, has taken years to write. Much of its content appeared originally as articles written over more than a decade. The project began as a way of making sense of the experience of working in human rights. In that work, I had the opportunity to meet many wonderful people who dedicate their lives to human rights. This work is dedicated to them and to those that will come after. The journey involved work on behalf of a network of human rights organisations as the Secretary of the Australian Forum of Human Rights Organisations and participation in international meetings, such as an NGO representative at the United Nations Commission on Human Rights.

As the end of the millennium approached, it could be seen that we had reached a kind of high-water mark. Human rights were in retreat. It was a strange observation, given that human rights laws and institutions had been elaborated across the world and were still being strengthened. In many places human rights are now found, as in the vision of Eleanor Roosevelt, in every school, college, farm and office. They appear in national and sub-national laws and in innumerable codes of conduct.

Yet the trouble was there. At the border attitudes were hardening. Tens of millions of refugees were being abandoned in human warehouses. It was a sign of things to come. The succeeding decades have not improved the picture. The carefully erected structure of international human rights instruments is a fragile repository for human rights: a precious and hard-won gift we inherit from previous generations. As much as human rights have contributed to a better present, they are constantly eroded and under threat of erosion. As time has progressed the attacks on human rights values have become more and more brazen. They have been mounted in the name of the nation, race, culture and domestic sovereignty.

In such a time there is a need to look more deeply at the human rights movement: to seek to better understand it.

Further, as the fiftieth anniversary of the Universal Declaration of Human Rights came and went in 1998, it became apparent that the movement did not know its own history, at least not very well. Of course, the international instruments and their making was known, but hardly if ever was there a deeper conversation about where the human rights movement came from and its history. This book is one effort to explore that story through a few of those whose lives "declared" the existence of human rights.

Those familiar with the literature will know that the topic of the history or "genealogy" of human rights has in recent years sparked a vigorous historical and philosophical debate. It is not my purpose to enter that debate and I do not write as a historian or philosopher. I write simply as a storyteller. What I see of the story is informed by the experience of having worked alongside human rights workers. From that vantage point, the signposts of the journey of human rights are readily recognisable in the historical record. Moreover, the stories told here are not told in the abstract. They are stories of real people, who shared our human condition. We try to see through their eyes. Without that human lens, human rights can hardly be understood.

Finally, a few words of acknowledgement. Firstly, a very warm thank you to Chris Sidoti for his kindness in writing the foreword to this volume. Also, to fellow writers in the Canberra Writers Group for their generous accompaniment in the craft of writing and suggestions that have helped to improve the finished work. Last but not least to my wife and family, who give everything meaning.

Introduction

You won't find the "official" story of human rights in the pages of this book. Indeed, most of the names you find here, barely appear in that *official* story. What you will discover, are the stories of those who have struggled against the oppressions and certainties of their own societies. Their lives, and the lives of many others like them, have given us human rights. They are in a sense the backstory of human rights: where human rights began. From their journeys, we learn what human rights *are*; and from them we learn what it means to work for human rights.

Paul Gilroy, in his oration *"Race and the Right to be Human"*, wrote:

> "The official genealogy ... [of human rights] ... is extremely narrow [and] is usually told ritualistically as a kind of

ethno-history. In that form, it contributes to a larger account of the moral and legal ascent of Europe and its civilizational offshoots. The bloody histories of colonization and conquest are rarely allowed to disrupt that linear, triumphalist tale of cosmopolitan progress. Struggles against racial or ethnic hierarchy are not viewed as an important source or inspiration for human rights movements and ideologies."[1]

As these words suggest, we won't find the deeper story of human rights in the obvious places. If we want to find the birth of human rights, we must look unflinchingly into the heart of the worst human oppressions. It is in that profound darkness that human rights appear: in the depths of colonialism, slavery, genocide, racism and the oppression of women.

Revolutions often created human rights instruments: the French Declaration of the Rights of Man; the US Declaration of Independence, are but two examples. Yet in such places the image is clouded. The French Revolution affirmed *brotherhood* among its mottos. Yet having eaten its own children, it spawned a continent-wide war and an oppressive tyrant. Among those

---

[1] Paul Gilroy, 2009

guillotined was Olympe de Gouges who had campaigned for abolition of slavery in the French colonies and, in her *1791 Declaration of the Rights of Woman and the Female Citizen,* for the rights of women. In the United States, it was *self-evident* that *all men are created equal,* yet slavery continued unabated. Such documents did not create human rights, and their championing of them, although marking historical watersheds, was far from perfect.

The stories told here unfold another kind of "Declaration of Human Rights" - the words not written on any sacred parchment - other than that of lives well lived. In their own way such stories are just as important as the Universal Declaration that was debated and formally adopted in 1948, although that Declaration crystallised what had gone before. The kind of Declaration written about here, has been inscribed countless times by the struggles of people like those that are described in this book. Struggles for a world which is more decent, more equal, more free, more kind, less fractious and less divided. You will find that in reading about these lives, you will come to know human rights far more profoundly than you would from a long reading of human rights treaties or rulings of international human rights bodies. This, at least, was my experience.

Here we look to ten people, their lives and work. Some of them are household names. Others are less known. Although each life is different, each of them saw the future long before many of those around them could. Moreover, they didn't just see the future; they worked to make it a reality. They all strived in one way or another for core ideals that today are enshrined in the Universal Declaration of Human Rights: *freedom, equality, dignity* and last, but not least, *fraternity,* or what we might today call *solidarity,* or as so well described by Martin Luther King Jr., *agape,* that universal love that includes all our fellow human beings.

Some struggled to promote the ideas that we now call human rights. Others worked to make those ideals a living reality. Each life enriches our understanding of what universal human rights mean. Virtually none of them would have called themselves human rights workers, and for some of them it was only one dimension of their lives and interests. Indeed, even the phrase *"human rights"* postdates some of their lives.

Together their lives span several centuries, cultures and backgrounds. They include men and women of diverse opinions, of religious belief (or none) and they spoke a variety of languages. They are in no sense representative of all who have directly or indirectly contributed to human rights. All the same, the story of their lives and the story of how human rights came to be, are intimately wound about.

The earliest whose contribution is explored in this book is Bartolome de Las Casas. He came to the Americas as a Spanish coloniser. But what his fellow colonists could not see, he could not deny. The original peoples of the Americas were his equals: they were human beings. Three hundred years after Las Casas, a young English scholar of Latin was confronted with the question of slavery. His Latin essay started him on a life's journey that led to the abolition of the Atlantic slave trade.

Lucretia Mott, who lived in the United States, saw the subjection of slaves and from struggling to free them she discovered the subjection of women. On the other side of the planet, at about the same time, another woman, Tahirih, a Persian poet, also saw the future, and she too sought the emancipation of women.

Frederick Douglass began life as a slave in the southern United States. He achieved freedom for himself and then dedicated his life to freedom for all. Alain Locke, two generations later, was an American philosopher. He helped create an African American cultural renaissance in the early twentieth century and his ideas influenced the civil rights movement that came after him.

Eleanor Roosevelt was the wife of a President. She rejected the segregation of her country, and her leadership helped give birth to the Universal Declaration of Human Rights.

Primo Levi was a young man when world war swept over him. Studying to be a chemist, the fact that his family was Jewish condemned him to Auschwitz. His writings made an important contribution to telling the story of the Holocaust.

The Reverend Dr Martin Luther King Jr. needs no introduction. The civil rights movement, of which he was a leader, took the ideals of human rights and made them a living reality for millions, not just in America, but around the world: not yet fully achieved, but the pathway that the world walked for most of the end of the twentieth century.

Albie Sachs was a judge of the Constitutional Court of South Africa. Before becoming a judge, he was a lawyer and dedicated his life to ending apartheid. He survived an attempt to assassinate him. He worked as a judge on the rebirth of his country and the healing of its wounds.

In what follows we will learn something of their lives and work. Where we can, we will use their own words to understand the better world they strived for; and the world they had to unmake. They are of course only a few of the many who have appeared and made substantial contributions to the cause of human rights. This work is an introduction to their stories.

Michael Curtotti

CHAPTER ONE
Bartolome de Las Casas

"All human beings are born free and equal in dignity and rights. They are endowed with reason and conscience and should act towards one another in a spirit of brotherhood."

1948 UNIVERSAL DECLARATION OF HUMAN RIGHTS,
ARTICLE 1

In 1492, when Bartolome de Las Casas was a boy aged just eight, the long Reconquista of Spain came to an end. Granada, the last Muslim kingdom fell, and King Ferdinand and Queen Isabella claimed the wonders of the Alhambra as their own. The human bonfires of the Spanish Inquisition had already begun. Among its targets would be the Jews and Muslims of Bartolome's country.

Yet in that same year an almost miraculous thing happened. A new world was discovered. A new world, which was there for the taking. At least, that was how those around him saw it. And in the beginning, Bartolome saw it the same way.

So, he joined the colonial expeditions to the Americas. In 1502, aged eighteen, he arrived on the island of Hispaniola (today Haiti and the Dominican Republic). It was almost the very beginning of the encounter between the Europeans and the people of the Americas.

But Las Casas did not find what he expected in the Americas. Unlike those around him, he soon reached the conclusion that nothing could justify what he and the other colonists were doing in the Americas. He was influenced by a group of Dominican preachers led by Antonio de Montesinos who in 1511 put the issues squarely before them:

> *"Tell me by what right of justice do you hold these Indians in such a cruel and horrible servitude? On what authority have you waged such detestable wars against these people who dealt quietly and peacefully on their own lands? Wars in which you have destroyed such an infinite number of them by homicides and slaughters never heard of before. Why do you keep them so oppressed and exhausted, without giving them enough to eat or curing them of the sicknesses they incur from*

the excessive labour you give them, and they die, or rather you kill them, in order to extract and acquire gold every day?"[2]

The colonists, rejecting these arguments, had the preachers recalled to Spain. Las Casas, however, became a Dominican. In 1513, he accompanied a military expedition to Cuba, where he personally witnessed the atrocities and, as a colonist, was awarded the usual plot of land and slaves with his friend Pablo de Renteria under the encomienda system. By 1514, when reading a passage from Ecclesiasticus, he concluded that both slavery and the conquests were wrong. He and his friend, who had reached the same conclusion, freed their slaves and sold their plot of land and Las Casas returned to Spain to appeal to the King.

He had started his life-long human rights campaign against the colonial abuses. To understand Las Casas' journey, it is useful to attempt to see what he saw. In order to present evidence to the King and others he records what was happening in the Americas in painful detail. The following provides some extracts from his work, ***A Brief Account of the Destruction of the Indies:***

"In the island of Hispaniola—which was the first, as we have said, to be invaded by the Christians—the immense massacres and destruction of these people began ... The [Indians] took up their weapons, which are poor enough

---

[2] Cited in George Sanderlin, pp 66-67

and little fitted for attack, being of little force and not even good for defence; For this reason, all their wars are little more than games with sticks, such as children play in our countries."

"The Christians, with their horses and swords and lances, began to slaughter and practise strange cruelty among them. They penetrated into the country and spared neither children nor the aged, nor pregnant women, nor those in child labour, all of whom they ran through the body and lacerated, as though they were assaulting so many lambs herded in their sheepfold.

"They made bets as to who would slit a man in two, or cut off his head at one blow: or they opened up his bowels. They tore the babes from their mothers' breast by the feet, and dashed their heads against the rocks. Others they seized by the shoulders and threw into the rivers, laughing and joking, and when they fell into the water they exclaimed: "boil body of so and so!" They spitted the bodies of other babes, together with their mothers and all who were before them, on their swords.

"They made a gallows just high enough for the feet to nearly touch the ground, and by thirteens, in honour and reverence of our Redeemer and the twelve Apostles, they put wood underneath and, with fire, they burned the Indians alive.

"They wrapped the bodies of others entirely in dry straw, binding them in it and setting fire to it; and so they *burned them. They cut off the hands of all they wished to take alive, made them carry them fastened on to them, and said: "Go and carry letters": that is; take the news to those who have fled to the mountains.*

"They generally killed the lords and nobles in the following way. They made wooden gridirons of stakes, bound them upon them, and made a slow fire beneath: thus the victims gave up the spirit by degrees, emitting cries of despair in their torture.

"I once saw that they had four or five of the chief lords stretched on the gridirons to burn them, and I think also there were two or three pairs of gridirons, where they were burning others; and because they cried aloud and annoyed the captain or prevented him sleeping, he commanded that they should strangle them: the officer who was burning them was worse than a hangman and did not wish to suffocate them, but with his own hands he gagged them, so that they should not make themselves heard, and he stirred up the fire, until they roasted slowly, according to his pleasure. I know his name, and knew also his relations in Seville. I saw all the above things and numberless others."[3]

We might disbelieve such obscene inhumanity; but for the fact that modern history has been punctuated with just such genocides. In writing out these accounts to the Spanish King, La Casas says:

---

[3] Cited in Francis Macnutt (trans.), p 318-321

> *"So as not to keep criminal silence concerning the ruin of numberless souls and bodies that these persons cause, I have decided to print some, though very few, of the innumerable instances I have collected in the past and can relate with truth, in order that Your Highness may read them …"*[4]

What Las Casas did, is what human rights workers have done ever since: collect evidence of human rights abuses and draw them to the attention of those in authority, so as to bring them to an end. What he records is the beginning of what is best described as an apocalypse that was to engulf the cities, towns and villages of the Americas. Horrifically, that colonial process, by which the countries of Europe subjugated most of the world, continued for 400 years. It swept across the world, in a slaughter, dispossession and violation of the rights of hundreds of millions. Las Casas makes its character clear to us.

> *"… in the said forty years, more than twelve million persons, men, and women, and children, have perished unjustly and through tyranny, by the infernal deeds and tyranny of the Christians; and I truly believe, nor think I am deceived, that it is more than fifteen.*
>
> *"Two ordinary and principal methods have the self-styled Christians, who have gone there, employed in extirpating these miserable nations and removing them from the face of the earth. The one, by unjust, cruel and*

---

[4] Cited in Francis Macnutt (trans.), p 312

tyrannous wars. The other, by slaying all those, who might aspire to, or sigh for, or think of liberty, or to escape from the torments that they suffer, such as all the native Lords, and adult men; for generally, they leave none alive in the wars, except the young men and the women, whom they oppress with the hardest, most horrible, and roughest servitude, to which either man or beast, can ever be put. To these two ways of infernal tyranny, all the many and divers other ways, which are numberless, of exterminating these people, are reduced, resolved, or sub-ordered according to kind.

"The reason why the Christians have killed and destroyed such infinite numbers of souls, is solely because they have made gold their ultimate aim, seeking to load themselves with riches in the shortest time and to mount by high steps, disproportioned to their condition: namely by their insatiable avarice and ambition, the greatest, that could be on the earth. These lands, being so happy and so rich, and the people so humble, so patient, and so easily subjugated, they have had no more respect, nor consideration nor have they taken more account of them (I speak with truth of what I have seen during all the aforementioned time) than,—I will not say of animals, for would to God they had considered and treated them as animals,—but as even less than the dung in the streets."[5]

---

[5] Cited in Francis Macnutt (trans.), p 316-318

Having set out a general description of the oppression the Spanish conquistadors were visiting on the Indians, Las Casas then details case after case where such methods were used, tracing the invasions from the Caribbean, to Mexico, Central America and Peru.

In every part of the Americas that the conquistadors reached, they would violently subjugate the people, generally committing brutal and genocidal massacres, extracting tributes of gold and then reducing what remained of the population to slavery. The Indians were brutally used for financial gain, for sport, as tools in the oppression of other Indian populations, as pack animals and even as food for the colonists' dogs.

Las Casas did all he could, not only to expose these abuses, but to change the situation. In 1542 his appeals to the King resulted in the *New Laws* which were designed to protect the Indians. Although the laws were flouted by the colonists, they sought to bring to an end the encomienda system, which was so oppressive to the Indians.

Before the Spanish Court, Las Casas famously debated both the injustice of the forcible conquest of the Indies, and the enslavement of the Indians. Such actions, he argued, were contrary both to divine and Spanish law. As Bishop of Chiapas in Central America, he denied his European parishioners absolution if they kept slaves. His long life was devoted to ameliorating and ending the human rights abuses he saw. His life has repeatedly drawn fruit. In the eighteenth century abolitionists recalled his work. In the nineteenth century South American liberation movements used his name. His name was associated with Liberation Theology in the twentieth century and the Latin American tradition of human rights in the twenty-first. It is also, perhaps, no coincidence, that the countries of the Americas where indigenous populations and cultures have best survived, are among those countries where Las Casas worked and focussed his attention.

The meeting between the Europeans and the peoples of the Americas in the sixteenth century raised a central issue: *what was the proper relationship between these two groups of people?* There was no history which could be used to justify oppression. Accordingly, its injustice was clear. Yet, as we have seen above, the colonists largely resolved this new relationship in terms of brutality, exploitation and subjugation. Las Casas saw things differently:

> *"All the races of the world are men, and of all men and of each individual there is but one definition, and this is that they are rational. All have understanding and will and free choice, as all are made in the image and likeness of God ... Thus the entire human race is one."*[6]

Like the later abolitionists of the eighteenth century who took as their slogan *"Am I not a man, and a brother?"* in their efforts to abolish the Atlantic slave trade, Las Casas upholds human equality and human fraternity. After the passage of centuries, such ideas were to eventually appear in the first article of the Universal Declaration of Human Rights, which has been quoted above.

Las Casas saw this hundreds of years before it was universally acknowledged. In part, his insight comes from the scholarly and religious traditions from which he

---

[6] Cited by Paul Carrozzo

comes. But just as surely, he realized it as a witness of human rights abuses. He saw it in the faces, lives and dignity of the Indians who he met, whom he repeatedly extolled and who helped him see how those traditions led to this answer. He was deeply ashamed of the conduct of his fellow colonists who called themselves "Christian"; but he held in high regard the civilised conduct of Indians who the Spaniard conquistadors so cruelly oppressed.

Yet even Las Casas made a serious mistake in his advocacy for the peoples of the Americas. In 1516 he spoke in favour of the African slave trade in order to save the Native Americans whom he saw being rapidly exterminated. Later he himself condemned the position he had earlier proposed. He came to see the taking of slaves as part of the African slave trade as unjust and tyrannical as the colonial genocide he campaigned against. In the last third of his life Las Casas was firmly against the slave trade. His words in 1516 and later did not create the slave trade, but he has been justly criticised for his early advocacy of it, and his words helped the trade to progress. As he came to know more of it, through a visit to Lisbon, then a centre of the slave trade, he saw it as no different to the oppression that he had seen in the Americas.

Las Casas teaches us not only of the good he did, but of the mistakes that can be made in the pursuit of a positive goal. Yet, he and others like him, at the birth of the colonialism of the modern era, showed there was another way. It took too long for most to understand.

The next great human rights struggle we will explore will take us forward centuries as new generations mobilised to end the Atlantic slave trade that in the era of Las Casas was just beginning.

CHAPTER TWO
Thomas Clarkson

"No one shall be held in slavery or servitude; slavery and the slave trade shall be prohibited in all their forms."

1948 UNIVERSAL DECLARATION OF HUMAN RIGHTS,

ARTICLE 4

In 1783 in Britain, and most of the world, slavery was an accepted and legal practice. Yet, in that year, an insurance case was heard before the British courts. The insurers claimed fraud. They had insured the cargo of the slave ship Zong, which carried African slaves from Africa to the Americas. They refused to pay a claim for "lost cargo". That lost cargo was more than 100 sick slaves who had been thrown overboard by the ship's captain, so that their value could be claimed against the insurers. If the slaves had died of natural causes (their sickness), no claim could be brought against the insurers. The insurers won their case. Efforts to bring murder charges against the ship owners failed. The slaves were not human beings; they were goods.

The realisation by a growing number of people of the horror of slavery, and the brutality of the slave trade led to action. Lawyers like Granville Sharp worked for changes to the law. Former slaves like Olaudah Equiano published their stories and worked for freedom. The Quakers had campaigned in North America and Britain against slavery for almost a century and they were prominent in the struggle. In 1783 British Quakers petitioned parliament for abolition of the trade.[7]

Thomas Clarkson was a student at Cambridge University, when in 1785, Peter Peckard, the Vice Chancellor of the university set a Latin Essay on the topic *Is it Right to Make Slaves of Others Against their Will?* Perhaps no more important question was ever put before the scholars of the university. A young man of twenty-four, Thomas

---

[7] It may be noted that Quakers are still active today in fields such as peace and human rights.

Clarkson entered the competition. He won. What he discovered in writing the essay was to change his life, for he devoted it to abolition of the slave trade. He and others, after a struggle of almost 20 years, achieved their goal and abolished the trade. Later he wrote of the effect the essay competition had on him:

> *"… the subject of it almost wholly engrossed my thoughts. I became at times very seriously affected while upon the road. I stopped my horse occasionally, and dismounted and walked. I frequently tried to persuade myself in these intervals that the contents of my Essay could not be true. The more however I reflected upon them, or rather upon the authorities on which they were founded, the more I gave them credit. Coming in sight of Wades Mill in Hertfordshire, I sat down disconsolate on the turf by the roadside and held my horse. Here a thought came into my mind, that if the contents of the Essay were true, it was time some person should see these calamities to their end. Agitated in this manner I reached home."*[8]

Shortly after the essay competition, Clarkson and others formed the *"Committee for the Abolition of the Slave Trade"* which began a sustained campaign for laws to ban the slave trade. Their work was one of the world's first true human rights campaigns and many of the techniques they used then are still basic to human rights work: letter

---

[8] Thomas Clarkson, chapter VII

campaigns, trade boycotts, submissions and petitions to parliament, collecting evidence of violations and distribution of promotional materials like medallions.

The campaign met with early success. It looked like Parliament would support the abolitionists. Then the slave industry mobilised against reform (as vested interests so often have). They claimed that slaves were well treated, that the slave trade didn't involve brutality, that the Africans were less human than others. Year after year they defeated the best efforts of the abolitionists. Parliamentarians supporting the cause, like William Wilberforce, were isolated and in a minority. The war against Napoleon intervened and the abolitionists were regarded with suspicion as potential revolutionaries. It was a long and bitter winter for the campaigners.

Yet eventually the war ended, and the campaign began again in earnest. Finally, in 1807, 18 years after the bill was first moved, the British Parliament adopted the Slave Trade Act, abolishing the slave trade. The same year, showing the international nature of the campaign, the United States Congress also adopted a bill abolishing the slave trade. Slavery itself, for the time-being, continued, but it had suffered a great blow.

Clarkson wrote a history of the abolition campaign. He explained why he felt it was important to write the account.

"For it cannot be otherwise than useful to us to know the

means which have been used, and the different persons who have moved, in so great a cause. It cannot be otherwise than useful to us to be impressively reminded of the simple axiom, which the perusal of this history will particularly suggest to us, that "the greatest works must have a beginning;" because the fostering of such an idea in our minds cannot but encourage us to undertake the removal of evils, however vast they may appear in their size, or however difficult to overcome. It cannot again be otherwise than useful to us to be assured (and this history will assure us of it) that in any work, which is a work of righteousness, however small the beginning may be, or however small the progress may be that we may make in it, we ought never to despair; for that, whatever checks and discouragements we may meet with, "no virtuous effort is ever ultimately lost." And finally, it cannot be otherwise than useful to us to form the opinion, which the contemplation of this subject must always produce, namely, that many of the evils, which are still left among us, may, by an union of wise and virtuous individuals, be greatly alleviated, if not entirely done away: for if the great evil of the Slave-trade, so deeply entrenched by its hundred interests, has fallen prostrate before the efforts of those who attacked it, what evil of a less magnitude shall not be more easily subdued?[9]

---

[9] Thomas Clarkson, chapter I

Clarkson's words give a sense of the magnitude of the struggle and the magnitude of the achievement. They also remind us that the achievement of social change begins with ordinary people doing what they can, but equally that the price of change is generations of dedicated work. Indeed, the abolitionists were relatively fortunate in taking only decades to defeat the Atlantic Slave Trade. Many human rights struggles have taken centuries, and many still continue. Even today slavery, although now illegal, continues in many unregulated and semi-regulated forms. Anti-Slavery continues to work against the practice and estimates that there are 40 million people in every country trapped in modern day slavery.[10] As terrible as such a figure is, had not generations worked to render the practice illegal, the situation would be worse. Yet much work remains to be done.

So far, we have only spoken of men. Yet many women were also abolitionists, working alongside their male colleagues. What these women discovered in working against slavery would make of them advocates for the equality and freedom of women.

---

[10] What is Modern Slavery https://www.antislavery.org/slavery-today/modern-slavery/ accessed 14 July 2020

CHAPTER THREE
Lucretia Mott

"States Parties condemn discrimination against women in all its forms, agree to pursue by all appropriate means and without delay a policy of eliminating discrimination against women and, to this end, undertake ... to embody the principle of the equality of men and women in their national constitutions or other appropriate legislation ..."

1978 UNITED NATIONS CONVENTION ON THE ELIMINATION
OF ALL FORMS OF DISCRIMINATION AGAINST WOMEN
ARTICLE 2

Lucretia Mott was born as the eighteenth century ended. She saw something that would take another century to begin to appear in the world. She dedicated much of her long life to working for the abolition of slavery and the emancipation of women. Her life and work, is among those which have shaped the world in which we live.

The significance of her contribution was recognised when, in 1923, Congresswoman Alice Paul first introduced the equal rights amendment to the US Congress calling it *'the Lucretia Mott amendment'*. The amendment, which has still not been adopted into the U.S. Constitution, states in its first draft article:

> *"Equality of rights under the law shall not be denied or abridged by the United States or by any state on account of sex."*

Lucretia Mott as Abolitionist

In the 1830s, before becoming an advocate for women's rights, Lucretia Mott was among the ranks of women who advocated the abolition of slavery in the United States. This involved her not only in supporting an unpopular cause, but also in challenging unwritten rules limiting the public role of women. Women were not accepted as public advocates. Such constraints were ones that were not part of her own background, coming from a Quaker community that had given her the role of religious minister, and employed her as a teacher.

In 1833, she participated in the founding of Philadelphia Female Anti-Slavery Society. As the 1830's moved on she was involved in the work of the Anti-Slavery Convention of American Women.

At the second meeting of the Convention in 1838, an angry mob gathered outside the Philadelphia Hall where the meeting was being held. Eventually the unrest forced the meeting to close. Lucretia Mott and white and black women participating in the Convention walked arm in arm through the mob, to prevent the black women being attacked. Later that night Philadelphia Hall, which had only been opened three days earlier, was burned to the ground by the mob.

The prevailing social attitudes against women's voices in mixed audiences is captured by the denial of a right to speak to one woman advocate which was put in the following terms by the chair.

> *"No woman shall speak or vote where I am moderator. I will not countenance such an outrage on decency. I will not consent to have women lord it over men in public assemblies. It is enough for women to rule at home ... Where woman's enticing eloquence is heard, men are incapable of right and efficient action. She beguiles men and blinds men by her smiles ... I had enough of woman's control in the nursery. Now I am a man, I will not submit to it."*[11]

---

[11] Cited in Jean Fagan Yellin and John C. Van Horne (eds.), p 242

The meeting supported this attitude, voting to silence Abbey Foster, an early abolitionist.

Lucretia Mott's leadership among abolitionists was reflected in her being asked to attend, along with her husband, James Mott, and three other women, as Philadelphia's representatives to the 1840 World Anti-Slavery Convention which was to be held in London. When she arrived there however, she and the other women were refused the right to speak, solely on the grounds of their gender.

The injustice of the decision from such a forum was underlined by some of the American male delegates, who spoke for their female fellow delegates. They argued that the women were critical to the abolitionist movement in America.

> *"If in the legislature [of Massachusetts] I have been able to do anything in the furtherance of this cause [abolition] ... it is mainly owing to the women ... My friend George Thompson, yonder, can testify to the faithful services rendered to this cause by those same women. He can tell you that when "gentlemen of property and standing," in broad day and broad cloth, undertook to drive him from Boston, putting his life in peril, it was our women who made their own persons a bulwark of protection around him. And shall such women be refused seats here?"*[12]

---

[12] Cited in Jean Fagan Yellin and John C. Van Horne (eds.), p 312

Lucretia Mott and the Emancipation of Women

It was at that Convention that Lucretia Mott met Elizabeth Cady Stanton, then a young woman. The experience of their exclusion served as a catalyst for action by Mott and Stanton. They decided to hold a convention when they returned home to advocate the rights of women.

By 1848, Mott and others had encouraged and joined Stanton in calling a conference at Seneca Falls (a remote town in upstate New York not far from Lake Ontario). That meeting marked the beginning of a formal American women's movement.

The meeting adopted the *"Declaration of Sentiments"*. It was framed to mirror the language of the U.S. Declaration of Independence and included a catalogue of deprivations, demanding among other things women's suffrage. Sixty-eight women signed the Declaration, including Mott herself, with the support of 38 men, including Frederick Douglass. Douglass was himself a leading African American campaigner for abolition, having himself escaped from slavery. We shall meet him in chapter five

The following illustrates the advocacy found in the *Declaration of Sentiments*:

> *"The history of mankind is a history of repeated injuries and usurpations on the part of man toward woman, having in direct object the establishment of an absolute*

tyranny over her. To prove this, let facts be submitted to a candid world.

He has never permitted her to exercise her inalienable right to the elective franchise.

He has compelled her to submit to laws, in the formation of which she had no voice.

He has withheld from her rights which are given to the most ignorant and degraded men – both natives and foreigners.

Having deprived her of this first right as a citizen, the elective franchise, thereby leaving her without representation in the halls of legislation, he has oppressed her on all sides.

He has taken from her all right in property, even to the wages she earns.

He has monopolized nearly all the profitable employments, and from those she is permitted to follow, she receives but a scanty remuneration.

He closes against her all the avenues to wealth and distinction, which he considers most honorable to himself. As a teacher of theology, medicine, or law, she is not known.

He has denied her the facilities for obtaining a thorough education – all colleges being closed against her.

He has endeavored, in every way that he could to destroy her confidence in her own powers, to lessen her self-

> *respect, and to make her willing to lead a dependent and abject life.*
>
> *Now, in view of this entire disfranchisement of one-half the people of this country, their social and religious degradation, – in view of the unjust laws above mentioned, and because women do feel themselves aggrieved, oppressed, and fraudulently deprived of their most sacred rights, we insist that they have immediate admission to all the rights and privileges which belong to them as citizens of these United States."*
>
> (extracts from the Declaration of Sentiments)

Apart from anything else, the Declaration gives us a clear picture of the legal and social deprivations of women that were considered normal and acceptable in nineteenth century American society.

Mott was to continue her advocacy of gender equality for many years, taking part in a stream of conventions and organizations working towards that goal. It was not until 1919 that women gained the vote in the United States. Lucretia, who had been born in 1793, did not live to see it, for she died in 1880. She had however lived long enough to see the vote extended to women in the then territory of Wyoming.

A New Female Identity

Some insight to Lucretia Mott's thought can be gained from her December 1849 Discourse on Women. She was conscious of the role of identity in the struggle for women's liberation.

She saw both women's self-conception and the conception of women imposed by society, as powerful barriers to women's progress.

It is sometimes claimed that human rights are peculiarly a product of Western culture. Yet the pursuit of human rights required figures like Lucretia Mott to challenge both accepted culture and law. Culture, as a general rule, has typically been a barrier to the progress of human rights. Consequently, the advance of human rights and a reform of culture go hand in hand, irrespective of the society involved. Further, it is important to note that human rights arose in the encounter of people from different parts of the world.

In the next chapter we discover a figure who in Persia, within her own cultural context, was a champion of the emancipation of women. She lived in the same era as Lucretia Mott. In the same year as the Declaration of Sentiments was debated in the state of New York, Tahirih called for the emancipation of women in a faraway part of the world.

CHAPTER FOUR
Tahirih

"Discrimination against women, denying or limiting as it does their equality of rights with men, is fundamentally unjust and constitutes an offence against human dignity. ... All appropriate measures shall be taken to abolish existing laws, customs, regulations and practices which are discriminatory against women, and to establish adequate legal protection for equal rights of men and women."

1967 DECLARATION ON THE ELIMINATION OF
DISCRIMINATION AGAINST WOMEN,
ARTICLES 1 AND 2

What we have seen of conditions in the United States were far from unique. Two hundred years ago, virtually everywhere in the world, women lived in legal, cultural and religious subjugation. It was a world so different to our own that it is difficult to imagine. In that world women had little role in public life, little opportunity for education and little opportunity to work, other than in the home. Although we should note that in the predominantly rural life that most of the people lived everywhere in the world, poorer women were often expected to work both inside and outside the home. In many countries, women did not have the right to own property. It was a world where women were typically subject to the legal control of male relatives and the law in the West, as much as the East, defended the right of husbands to beat and control their wives.

Tahirih was born into this world and she was one of the heralds of the emancipation of women. She was born around 1814 or 1817 in the city of Qazvin in Iran. Her father was a prominent religious cleric. Unusually, he educated his daughter. As she grew, so did the fame of her knowledge of sacred texts and insight. Despite the constraints under which she was placed as a woman — she entered public discourse — famously defeating male scholars in debate while speaking from behind a curtain. (This was all that was permitted to her).

As was the lot of many women of her time, she was married at a young age. Although she had three children, the marriage was unhappy, and she separated from her husband.

Notwithstanding the discouragement of her family she became interested in and then a defender of new religious ideas: in particular a school of thinking which anticipated the imminent arrival of a new messenger of God. Her brother-in-law, who shared her viewpoint was one of those who, in 1844, was setting out to search for the new messenger. So strong was her belief that she gave him a letter confessing her faith, to be handed to the new messenger as soon as he was found. As a result of this letter, Tahirih became one of the Apostles of the Bab, the first prophet of the Babi, and later the Baha'i Faith.

Although she never met the Bab, she soon became a prominent teacher of the new beliefs, attracting a growing following in Iraq, where she was then living. The local Islamic clergy, hostile to her growing influence, agitated to have her placed under house arrest and eventually brought about her expulsion back to Iran.

In 1848, a first conference of the Babis was held in the village of Badasht, near the southern shore of the Caspian Sea. Tahirih was one of its most prominent participants – and her actions at the conference is one of the most well-known incidents of her life.

An unresolved topic of debate was how deeply the new faith would depart from the traditions, concepts and practices of the society around them. One day, Tahirih appeared at the conference unveiled, announcing "the trumpet has been blown" – quoting words from the Qur'an which symbolised the arrival of a new era and the end of the old. Some, clinging to traditional concepts, were scandalized, viewing her unveiled appearance as indecent. Others understood the significance. Her view was to prevail.

Not long after the conference, Tahirih was arrested by government authorities and brought back to Tehran, where she was placed under house arrest for what remained of her life. Her reputation and esteem were such that the Shah, having seen her after her return, offered to marry her, but on condition that she would deny her faith. Her poetic reply was:

> Kingdom, wealth and ruling be for thee,
>
> Wandering, becoming a poor dervish and calamity be for me.
>
> If that station is good, let it be for thee,
>
> And if this station is bad, I long for it, let it be for me![13]

Despite her house arrest she continued to draw visitors (including women of the court) who wanted to hear her words. In addition to her religious knowledge she became famed for her poetry.

The next few years were horrific ones for the Babi community. The clergy of Iran, fuelling religious fanaticism, caused the Babis to be attacked wherever they were found. The Babis defended themselves. These conflicts all ended the same way: the defeat and extermination of thousands of Babis. Sometimes after a

---

[13] Martha Root, p 69

heroic but hopeless struggle, often accompanied by horrific public tortures and executions, the Babi community virtually disappeared.

The home in which Tahirih was imprisoned

In 1852 a new wave of persecution was to also take Tahirih's life. Martha Root, an American woman to whom Tahirih was an inspiration, visited Tahirih's birthplace in Persia early in the twentieth century and recorded the following.

> *The relative of Táhirih in Qazvin told me that the day before her martyrdom she was called to the presence of His Imperial Majesty Násiri'd-Din Sháh. He said to her that day: "Why should you be a believer in the Báb?" She replied not with her own words, but from the Qu'rán which was about as follows, that I do not worship whom you worship, and you do not worship whom I worship. I shall never worship whom you worship and you will never worship whom I worship. Therefore, permit that I worship whom I wish and you*

worship whom you wish.

His Majesty bent his head in silence for some time and then arose and left the room without saying anything. However, I heard that the eunuch and others around the Sháh were determined she should be killed, and the next day they had her murdered without the Sháh's knowledge; and he was very grieved when he learned of it.[14]

Martha Root also records another slightly different account:

"Wishing to accomplish her downfall, the chiefs of the government commanded Háji Mullá Kani and Háji Mullá Muhammad Andirmáni, two of the most learned and famous clergymen of Tihrán, to discuss with her and declared that whatever these two Muslim divines decided upon should be done.

"Accordingly discussions were held in the home [where she was imprisoned]. In every meeting she debated with them and they were defeated; still they remained unconvinced and finally wrote a sentence as follows: 'This woman is astray and a leader astray of others; therefore, her death is necessary and expedient.' The government accepted this, added some false charges to it and spread it broadcast among men and women. Thus all were anticipating her death. However,

---

[14] Martha Root, p 70

notwithstanding the proclamation, through fear they killed her secretly by night.

Tahirih knew she was about to be killed. When her executioners arrived, she had dressed herself in a costly dress. Abdu'l Baha told the story of her last moments.

"They brought her into a garden, where the headsmen waited; but these wavered and then refused to end her life. A slave was found, far gone in drunkenness; besotted, vicious, black of heart. And he strangled Táhirih. He forced a scarf between her lips and rammed it down her throat. Then they lifted up her unsullied body and flung it in a well, there in the garden, and over it threw down earth and stones …"[15]

As has been noted by one observer – the secretiveness with which her life was ended was in marked contrast to the public and grotesque torture and execution imposed on other Babi victims caught up in the same wave of persecution. Her death has not silenced her voice. Her poetry is famed around the world.

"I would explain all my grief

Dot by dot, point by point

If heart to heart we talk

And face to face we meet.

To catch a glimpse of thee

---

[15] Abdu'l Baha, p 355

I am wandering like a breeze

From house to house, door to door

Place to place, street to street.

In separation from thee

The blood of my heart gushes out of my eyes

In torrent after torrent, river after river

Wave after wave, stream after stream.

This afflicted heart of mine

Has woven your love

To the stuff of life

Strand by strand, thread to thread.[16]

She inspired and continues to inspire generations after her. Martha Root — herself an astonishing pioneer — held her as a role model. She writes of the many men and women alike who paid tribute to her:

> *Marianna Hainisch of Vienna, Austria, mother of the President of Austria when I visited her in 1925, said to me: "The greatest ideal of womanhood all my life has been Táhirih (Qurratu'l-'Ayn) of Qazvin, Irán. I was only seventeen years old when I heard of her life and her martyrdom, but I said: "I shall try to do for the women of Austria what Táhirih gave her life to do for women of Persia.'" No woman in Austria has done so much for*

---

[16] Susan Gammage, item 3

freedom and education for women as has Mrs Hainisch.[17]

Today, Tahirih is recognised as the founder of the women's movement in Iran. Muhammad Iqbal, a poet philosopher whose work is revered in Pakistan was also one of her admirers. He wrote:

"Think not that Tahirih has left this world.

Rather she is present in the very conscience of her age."[18]

Tahirih's famous final words to her executioners were:

"You can kill me as soon as you like, but you cannot stop the emancipation of women."[19]

* * *

We now return to the United States, to look at the life of a man who was himself a slave. He freed himself from slavery, but millions of his brothers and sisters remained enslaved in the country of his birth. Their freedom became his cause.

---

[17] Martha Root, p 86

[18] Sabir Afaqi and Jan T Jasion, p 31

[19] Shoghi Effendi, p 75

CHAPTER FIVE
Frederick Douglass

"All are equal before the law and are entitled without any discrimination to equal protection of the law."

1948 UNIVERSAL DECLARATION OF HUMAN RIGHTS, ARTICLE 6

Frederick Douglass was a remarkable worker for human rights. Although he lived more than a century ago, his thoughts remain pressingly relevant.

He began life as a slave, but winning his own freedom, he fought not only for abolition of slavery but also gave his support to other human rights causes, such as the emancipation of women.

Born in 1818 in Talbot County, Maryland, he was separated from his mother at an early age. This, he writes, as was typically done with slave children. His father, he believed, was his mother's master. Even though it was against the law for slave children to be taught to read and write, Sophia Auld, the wife of one of his master's brothers, began his education. When it was discovered, a stop was put to it, but Douglass found opportunities to continue to learn on his own. The fact that it was forbidden told Douglass that 'knowledge is the pathway to freedom'. While still enslaved he used his knowledge to secretly teach fellow slaves to read the Bible, until their meetings were discovered.

Douglass' opportunity to escape came when, due to his skills, he was hired out by his master to work for wages. The wages were however paid not to him, but to his master. Douglass worked at caulking ships and on 3 September 1838 he escaped, disguised as a free sailor, bearing the false documents of a free man.

These small details of slavery tell us how it was systematically maintained, the oppressed kept in their servitude by both legal and non-legal devices.

After his escape, Douglass settled in Massachusetts and was quickly drawn into Abolitionist circles. In 1845 he published his first autobiography telling the story of his early life and escape to freedom. Fearing laws which might allow his legal master to claim his 'property' back, Douglass decided to seek a safer refuge across the sea in Ireland. It was to him an entirely different world.

> *"I breathe, and lo! the chattel [slave] becomes a man. I gaze around in vain for one who will question my equal humanity, claim me as his slave, or offer me an insult. I employ a cab – I am seated beside white people – I reach the hotel – I enter the same door – I am shown into the same parlour – I dine at the same table – and no one is offended ... I find myself regarded and treated at every turn with the kindness and deference paid to white people."*[20]

Supporters raised funds to purchase the legal title of Frederick Douglass from his master. Finally, a legally free man, he returned to the United States. In 1848 we find him as the sole African American present at the Seneca Falls Conference which called for the emancipation of women. His life was one of public service and advocacy for the human rights of African Americans, both before and after the civil war.

Let us turn for inspiration to the words of Frederick Douglass, written in his fight against chattel slavery, for

---

[20] Frederick Douglass (1), p 173

surely his words affirm that all human beings are equal. When he spoke, chattel slavery was still an accepted institution in the southern states of the United States.

The Meaning of July Fourth for the Negro by Frederick Douglass, 1852 Rochester, New York

Fellow Citizens, I am not wanting in respect for the fathers of this republic. The signers of the Declaration of Independence were brave men. They were great men, too great enough to give frame to a great age. ... They were statesmen, patriots and heroes, and for the good they did, and the principles they contended for, I will unite with you to honor their memory....

...Fellow-citizens, pardon me, allow me to ask, why am I called upon to speak here to-day? What have I, or those I represent, to do with your national independence? Are the great principles of political freedom and of natural justice, embodied in that Declaration of Independence, extended to us? and am I, therefore, called upon to bring our humble offering to the national altar, and to confess the benefits and express devout gratitude for the blessings resulting from your independence to us?

Would to God, both for your sakes and ours, that an affirmative answer could be truthfully returned to these questions! Then would my task be light, and my burden easy and delightful. For who is there so cold, that a nation's sympathy could not warm him? Who so obdurate and dead to the claims of gratitude, that would not thankfully acknowledge such priceless benefits? Who so stolid and selfish, that would not give his voice to swell the hallelujahs of a nation's jubilee, when the chains of servitude had been torn from his limbs? I am not that man. In a case like that, the dumb might eloquently speak, and the "lame man leap as an hart."

But such is not the state of the case. I say it with a sad sense of the disparity between us. I am not included within the pale of glorious anniversary! Your high independence only reveals the immeasurable distance between us. The blessings in which you, this day, rejoice, are not enjoyed in common. The rich inheritance of justice, liberty, prosperity and independence, bequeathed by your fathers, is shared by you, not by me. The sunlight that brought light and healing to you, has brought stripes and death to me. This Fourth July is yours, not mine. You may rejoice, I must mourn. To drag a man in fetters into the grand illuminated temple of liberty, and call upon him to join you in joyous anthems, were inhuman mockery and sacrilegious irony. Do you mean, citizens, to mock me, by asking me to speak to-day? If so, there is a parallel to your conduct. And let me warn you that it is dangerous to copy the example of a nation whose crimes, towering up to heaven, were thrown down by the breath of the Almighty, burying that nation in irrevocable ruin! I can to-day take up the plaintive lament of a peeled and woe-smitten people!

"By the rivers of Babylon, there we sat down. Yea! we wept when we remembered Zion. We hanged our harps upon the willows in the midst thereof. For there, they that carried us away captive, required of us a song; and they who wasted us required of us mirth, saying, Sing us one of the songs of Zion. How can we sing the Lord's song in a strange land? If I forget thee, O Jerusalem, let my right hand forget her cunning. If I do not remember thee, let my tongue cleave to the roof of my mouth."

"Fellow-citizens, above your national, tumultuous joy, I hear the mournful wail of millions! whose chains, heavy and grievous yesterday, are, to-day, rendered more intolerable by the jubilee shouts that reach them. If I do forget, if I do not faithfully remember those bleeding children of sorrow this day, "may my right hand forget her cunning, and may my tongue cleave to the roof of my mouth!" To forget them, to pass lightly over their wrongs, and to chime in with the popular theme, would be treason most scandalous and shocking, and would make me a reproach before God and the world. My subject, then, fellow-citizens, is American slavery. I shall see this day and its popular characteristics from the slave's point of view. Standing there identified with the American bondman, making his wrongs mine, I do not hesitate to declare, with all my soul, that the character and conduct of this nation never looked blacker to me than on this 4th of July! Whether we turn to the declarations of the past, or to the professions of the present, the conduct of the *nation seems equally hideous and revolting. America is false to the past, false to the present, and solemnly binds herself to be false to the future. Standing with God and the crushed and bleeding slave on this occasion, I will, in the name of humanity which is outraged, in the name of liberty which is fettered, in the name of the constitution and the Bible which are disregarded and trampled upon, dare to call in question and to denounce, with all the emphasis I can command, everything that serves to perpetuate slavery is the great sin and shame of America! "I will not equivocate; I will not excuse"; I will use the severest language I can command; and yet not one word shall escape me that any man, whose judgment is not blinded by prejudice, or who is not at heart a slaveholder, shall not confess to be right and just.*

"... For the present, it is enough to affirm the equal manhood of the Negro race. Is it not astonishing that, while we are ploughing, planting, and reaping, using all kinds of mechanical tools, erecting houses, constructing bridges, building ships, working in metals of brass, iron, copper, silver and gold; that, while we are reading, writing and ciphering, acting as clerks, merchants and secretaries, having among us lawyers, doctors, ministers, poets, authors, editors, orators and teachers; that, while we are engaged in all manner of enterprises common to other men, digging gold in California, capturing the whale in the Pacific, feeding sheep and cattle on the hillside, living, moving, acting, thinking, planning, living in

families as husbands, wives and children, and, above all, confessing and worshipping the Christian's God, and looking hopefully for life and immortality beyond the grave, we are called upon to prove that we are men!

"Would you have me argue that man is entitled to liberty? that he is the rightful owner of his own body? You have already declared it. Must I argue the wrongfulness of slavery? Is that a question for Republicans? Is it to be settled by the rules of logic and argumentation, as a matter beset with great difficulty, involving a doubtful application of the principle of justice, hard to be understood? How should I look to-day, in the presence of Americans, dividing, and subdividing a discourse, to show that men have a natural right to freedom? speaking of it relatively and positively, negatively and affirmatively. To do so, would be to make myself ridiculous, and to offer an insult to your understanding. There is not a man beneath the canopy of heaven that does not know that slavery is wrong for him.

"What, am I to argue that it is wrong to make men brutes, to rob them of their liberty, to work them without wages, to keep them ignorant of their relations to their fellow men, to beat them with sticks, to flay their flesh with the lash, to load their limbs with irons, to hunt them with dogs, to sell them at auction, to sunder their families, to knock out their teeth, to burn their flesh, to starve them into obedience and submission to their masters? Must I argue that a system thus marked with blood, and stained

with pollution, is wrong? No! I will not. I have better employment for my time and strength than such arguments would imply.

"... What, to the American slave, is your 4th of July? I answer; a day that reveals to him, more than all other days in the year, the gross injustice and cruelty to which he is the constant victim. To him, your celebration is a sham; your boasted liberty, an unholy license; your national greatness, swelling vanity; your sounds of rejoicing are empty and heartless; your denunciation of tyrants, brass fronted impudence; your shouts of liberty and equality, hollow mockery; your prayers and hymns, your sermons and thanksgivings, with all your religious parade and solemnity, are, to Him, mere bombast, fraud, deception, impiety, and hypocrisy — a thin veil to cover up crimes which would disgrace a nation of savages. There is not a nation on the earth guilty of practices more shocking and bloody than are the people of the United States, at this very hour.

"Go where you may, search where you will, roam through all the monarchies and despotisms of the Old World, travel through South America, search out every abuse, and when you have found the last, lay your facts by the side of the everyday practices of this nation, and you will say with me, that, for revolting barbarity and shameless hypocrisy, America reigns without a rival....

"...Allow me to say, in conclusion, notwithstanding the dark picture I have this day presented, of the state of the

nation, I do not despair of this country. There are forces in operation which must inevitably work the downfall of slavery. "The arm of the Lord is not shortened," and the doom of slavery is certain. I, therefore, leave off where I began, with hope. While drawing encouragement from "the Declaration of Independence," the great principles it contains, and the genius of American Institutions, my spirit is also cheered by the obvious tendencies of the age. Nations do not now stand in the same relation to each other that they did ages ago. No nation can now shut itself up from the surrounding world and trot round in the same old path of its fathers without interference. The time was when such could be done. Long established customs of hurtful character could formerly fence themselves in, and do their evil work with social impunity. Knowledge was then confined and enjoyed by the privileged few, and the multitude walked on in mental darkness. But a change has now come over the affairs of mankind ..."

Frederick Douglass's words were spoken in 1852. However, in little over a decade the Civil War would demolish slavery. It must have seemed a confirmation of his confidence. Yet the promise of a new era was to be in many ways still-born, despite the rivers of blood shed in the conflict. Within decades, new methods of oppression had been developed and enforced.

In 1883 Frederick Douglass in a speech said:

"While a slave there was a mountain of gold on his breast

to keep him down— now that he is free there is a mountain of prejudice to hold him down."[21]

By 1888 he was even more bleak.

"Take his relation to the national government and we shall find him a deserted, a defrauded, a swindled, and an outcast man. In law, free; in fact, a slave. In law, a citizen; in fact, an alien; in law, a voter; in fact, a disenfranchised man. In law his color is no crime; in fact, his color exposes him to be treated as a criminal. Toward him every attribute of a just government is contradicted."[22]

In a sign of worse things to come, his second marriage to Helen Pitts after the death of his first wife Anna Murray two years earlier, was widely condemned for "crossing the color line".

"People who had remained silent over the unlawful relations of the white slave masters with their colored slave women loudly condemned me for marrying a wife a few shades lighter than myself. They would have no objection to my marrying a person much darker in complexion than myself, but to marry one much lighter and of the complexion of my father rather than of that of my mother, was, in the popular eye, a shocking offense, and one for which I was to be ostracized by white and black alike."[23]

---

[21] Frederick Douglass (2), p 176
[22] Frederick Douglass (2), p 176
[23] Frederick Douglass (2), p 177

In his final autobiography, he records a death bed meeting that happened at the request of his former master, and possible father, when Douglass happened to be in the same town. This man, whose criminal and brutal behaviour over many years Douglass had mercilessly exposed, now appears again in a moving scene of reconciliation and forgiveness. This event was undoubtedly personally significant to Douglass himself. But it has a wider importance, for he shares the meeting with his readers, and we can conclude that he has a purpose in doing so. His enemy, his words conveyed in that meeting, was not any human being, but the institution of slavery itself.[24]

As the old century ended and the new began, in former slave states the African American population remained marginalised and impoverished. The Jim Crow era of segregation of African Americans strengthened its grip and became national policy. Scientific racism provided a new justification for policies and laws such as the "one drop" rule,[25] and increasingly institutionalised racism against the mixed race population of America. Intermarriage between "races" became a "genetic" crime, in an increasing number of states. In this era, Alain Locke arose and undertook his work.

---

[24] Frederick Douglass (3), pp 536-538

[25] In the laws and practices of the era, one drop of African American blood (i.e. family heritage) was considered "polluting", and meant the owner would be classified as negro, and therefore to be segregated from the white population.

CHAPTER SIX
Alain Locke

"Everyone has the right freely to participate in the cultural life of the community, to enjoy the arts and to share in scientific advancement and its benefits."

1948 UNIVERSAL DECLARATION OF HUMAN RIGHTS,
ARTICLE 27(1))

At the heart of Alain Locke's work is the idea that identity and oppression are connected with each other: that the pathway to emancipation is through re-imagining identity. Early on he explored these themes in the introduction he wrote to the 1925 anthology of African American literature and art titled *"The New Negro"*.

Of Alain Locke,[26] Martin Luther King Jr. said:

> *"We're going to let our children know that the only philosophers that lived were not Plato and Aristotle, but W.E.B. Du Bois and Alain Locke came through the universe."*[27]

This tribute, particularly from Martin Luther King, calls for greater attention to Alain Locke's philosophy and contribution. Alain Locke is well known to the scholars who have studied his life. On 13 September 2014, an interment ceremony was held for his ashes at the U.S. Congressional Cemetery. Forgotten, his ashes had been stored away in a university drawer for 60 years. The ceremony is a hopeful sign that the world was beginning to pay renewed attention to Alain Locke's thoughts.

Much could be said about his life and career as a writer, philosopher, and race equality advocate. He was the first

---

[26] The painting of Alaine Locke by Betsy Graves Reyneau, 1888-1964
[27] Alain Locke Scholarship Hertford College University of Oxford, https://www.hertford.ox.ac.uk/support-us/fundraising-priorities/alain-locke-senior-scholarship

African American Rhodes Scholar and he became a professor of philosophy at Howard University. He was an advocate of racial equality from early in his life. Indeed, he was among the first to challenge the notion that 'race' was a fixed biological reality. He correctly saw 'race' as a socially constructed and fluid cultural artefact, at a time when most of the western world, including its leading thinkers, were subscribing to theories of scientific racism. His experience of oppression as an African American pursuing a life as a scholar was a major influence in his life. Another important influence on his thought was the Baha'i Faith, of which he was a member, and from which he drew an increasingly universalist philosophy as his work unfolded.

Here we will focus on his insights about identity. Essentially, the point that Alain Locke makes in the introduction to *The New Negro*, is that how we and others see ourselves is central to our emancipation. It was an insight born in the experience of racial discrimination and segregation.

It is possible that the women's movement influenced Alain Locke's thoughts on this point, as there is a similar thread in first wave and later feminism. It may be however that the parallel is simply a shared insight arising from parallel experiences of oppression.

Alain Locke and *The New Negro*

The New Negro explores identity by anticipating, proclaiming and furthering an intellectual and cultural flowering among African Americans known as the "Harlem Renaissance". The Renaissance was an artistic and cultural movement that flourished in Harlem in the pre-war years until the Great Depression and other factors brought the movement to an end.

Locke expressed his concept as follows:

> *"... the Old Negro had long become more of a myth than a man. The Old Negro, we must remember, was a creature of moral debate and historical controversy. His has been a stock figure perpetuated as an historical fiction partly in innocent sentimentalism, partly in deliberate reactionism. "... So for generations in the mind of America, the Negro has been more of a formula than a human being — a something to be argued about, condemned or defended, to be "kept down," or "in his place," or "helped up," to be worried with or worried over, harassed or patronized, a social bogey or a social burden. The thinking Negro even has been induced to share this same general attitude, to focus his attention on controversial issues, to see himself in the distorted perspective of a social problem. His shadow, so to speak, has been more real to him than his personality. ... Little true social or self-understanding has or could come from such a situation ..."*[28]

---

[28] Cited in Charles Molesworth (ed), p 442

Although exploring its dimensions, Locke doesn't try to create or impose a rigid definition of what the 'New Negro' should be. As he says, he leaves this task to the rising generation.

The New Negro primarily showcases a diversity of African American art, culture and literature, from traditional negro spirituals and their influence on American music, to the philosophy of W.E.B. Du Bois. Through art and culture, *The New Negro* manifests a new identity that demolishes racist myths and limiting self-conceptions that served to keep African Americans in subjugation.

The New Negro was a powerful intellectual and cultural response to the Jim Crow era, with its lynchings, its scientific racism, its "race hygiene", its social Darwinism, its criminalization of "race mixing" and its entrenchment of legal segregation.

Locke contributed in other ways on the question of identity. As suggested above, he was a trenchant critic of scientific racism, using reason and philosophy to attack claims around race and culture that lacked scientific validity.[29]

In Locke's 1950 retrospective on *the New Negro* and its associated movement, he reflects both on what he meant, and where he thought identity might trend. As he does so however, he draws his readers attention to the difficulty

---

[29] Leonard Harris, pp 164 and following

of defining "Negro art", based on a constructed racial category that ultimately must remain contingent and shifting. He states of the movement that:

> *"From the beginning racial chauvinism was supposed to be ruled out; five of the collaborators of The New Negro were whites whose readily accepted passport was competent understanding of the cultural objectives of the movement and creative participation in them. The substance of Negro life was emphasized, not its complexion. ...*
>
> *"So far as the emancipation of the public mind from prejudice and group stereotypes, this may be properly regarded as ... a new Negro contribution to the broadening of the nation's culture. But for us as Negroes, it is even more important to realize how necessary it is to share understandingly and participate creatively in these promising enlargements of the common mind and spirit. To be democratic is as important is it is to be treated democratically; democracy is a two-way process and accomplishment ..."*[30]

Stretching the Social Mind

We see more of Locke's thought in the 1944 commencement address titled "Stretching our Social Mind" which Alain Locke delivered at the Hampton Institute (now Hampton University), Virginia. He returns

---

[30] Leonard Harris, pp 230 and following

to the issues of identity at a group level.

> *"Part of the lot of any oppressed or persecuted minority is an acute and sometimes morbid social consciousness. To this the Negro is no exception. One of the most important issues before us as a racial group today is to broaden our deep but often too narrow group consciousness and channel it toward the progressive goals and movements of these modern times. Neither reactionary, subservient inter-racialism of the traditional sort nor narrow chauvinistic racialism are a proper and adequate base for our present-day thinking or our present-day group planning and action. It is high time, therefore, to stretch our social minds and achieve thereby a new dynamic as well as new alliances in the common fight for human justice and freedom of which our minority cause is a vital but nonetheless only a fractional part.*
>
> *"... just as world-mindedness must dominate and remould nation-mindedness, so we must transform eventually race-mindedness into human-mindedness. Today it is possible and necessary for Negroes to conceive their special disabilities as flaws in the general democratic structure. The intelligent and effective righting of our racial wrongs and handicaps involves pleading and righting the cause of any and all oppressed minorities. In making common cause with all such broader issues, we shall find that we strengthen, both*

morally and practically, our own."[31]

As Locke pointed to a reshaping of African American identity to seize the 'high ground' of arts and culture in the 1920's as a response to oppressive stereotypes, in the 1940s, he again suggests a re-framing – the conscious creation of a social identity concerned with collective human emancipation. Here was another high ground.

In this journey, Locke takes African American identity from that of victims of racial oppression to leaders in human emancipation.

Alain Locke's Influence

That Locke's thoughts and teaching had real world impact, we need merely look at Martin Luther King Jr., who in his work, did exactly what Alain Locke had advocated. When in 1965 President Johnson introduced *the Voting Rights Act* and presented the pen used to sign the Voting Rights Act into law, to Martin Luther King Jr., it was a tribute to the contribution that African Americans had made to the life of America. It was an actualization of Locke's vision. As President Johnson said:

> *"The real hero of this struggle is the American Negro. His actions and protests, his courage to risk safety, and even to risk his life, have awakened the conscience of this*

---

[31] Christopher Buck and Betty Fisher (eds.)

nation. His demonstrations have been designed to call attention to injustice, designed to provoke change; designed to stir reform. He has been called upon to make good the promise of America. And who among us can say that we would have made the same progress were it not for his persistent bravery and his faith in American democracy?"[32]

It is notable that such creative use of identity to advance human rights has been largely muted in today's human rights discourse. The question of identity and the contribution it might make in the context of human rights in the twenty-first century is deserving of renewed thought and attention.

However, as we have already seen in Alaine Locke's time, a very different and destructive idea of identity had grown in influence during his lifetime. The scientific racism against which he struggled, which defined human identity in terms of "genes" and "race", had its proponents also on the other side of the Atlantic. Such race science, together with eugenics, taken up by German and Italian thinkers, exploded in a new and more virulent form. This "scientific" doctrine held that a person's value was to be judged only by their genes. The doctrine of survival of the fittest would justify the pursuit of policies to ensure the racially defined "fittest" would survive. Laws, drawing on models in America, would be framed

---

[32] Cited in Nick Kotz, p 311

to maintain "racial purity". The "Nordic" and "Aryan" "race" (a genetic rather than national category) was to be marked out to inherit the Earth. Hundreds of millions, classified as sub-human, would only be fit for enslavement and extermination.[33] In this world, our next figure, Primo Levi, found himself on the wrong side of the genetic line.

---

[33] For an incisive portrayal, including a discussion of the links between racist doctrine in North America and Europe see, Edwin Black. James Whitman is another source which explores the Nazi use of racist legislation in the United States as models for the development of Germany's Nuremberg Laws which stripped Jews of citizenship. See Joshua Zimmerman for the situation in Italy.

CHAPTER SEVEN
Primo Levi

"The Contracting Parties confirm that genocide, whether committed in time of peace or in time of war, is a crime under international law which they undertake to prevent and to punish."

1948 UNITED NATIONS CONVENTION ON THE PREVENTION AND PUNISHMENT OF THE CRIME OF GENOCIDE, ARTICLE 1

Primo Levi might have led an unexceptional life as an Italian chemist had not his background marked him out for persecution.

Even though Italy's past had seen periodic outbreaks of anti-semitism stretching back to ancient times, when in the 1860s, the Italian state was born, what was to happen to Italy's Jews in World War 2 was almost unimaginable.

Newborn, the Italian state rejected the ignorance and prejudice of the past. The Jewish ghettoes were abolished across Italy and Jews welcomed as equal citizens. Indeed, at the time, Italy was one of the most favourable environments in Europe for its Jewish community. Jews had been among the supporters and leaders of the cause of Italian unification. Eight had been among Garibaldi's Thousand who landed in Sicily and some appeared in the heroic registers of World War 1. Alessandro Fortis who, had fought with Garibaldi in the wars of liberation, became Italy's first Jewish Prime Minister in 1905. In 1910, Luigi Luzzatti took office as Italy's second Jewish Prime Minister. Such circumstances made what was to happen later even more horrific.

In Saul Steinberg's words, Italy was their "lost paradise". In the impoverished area of Rome's former Jewish ghetto, integration lagged, but it was the exception. Across Italy intermarriage was high at an average of 43%. In cities such as Trieste and Milan it reached the high 50s.

Even in the early years of the Fascist regime, Italy's Jewish population of 46,000 (less than one in a thousand Italians) was not targeted, as was to occur later. In those early years some were even members of the Fascist party. As late as 1932 Mussolini was quoted as trenchantly opposed to ideas of (biological) racism.

> *"Of course there are no pure races left; not even the Jews ... Race! It is a feeling, not a reality; ninety-five percent, at least, it is a feeling. Nothing will ever make me believe that biologically pure races can be shown to exist today. Amusingly enough, not one of those who have proclaimed the nobility of the Teutonic race was himself a Teuton ... No such doctrine will ever find wide acceptance here in Italy ... National pride has no need of the delirium of race ... Anti-semitism does not exist in Italy ... Italians of Jewish birth have shown themselves good citizens, and they fought bravely in the war. Many of them occupy leading position in the universities, in the army, in the banks. Quite a few of them are generals; General Modena is commandant of Sardinia."*[34]

However, the statement was evasive and intended to deflect Emil Ludwig, a probing journalist who was enquiring into the absence of Jews in the Academy of Italy.

Although Mussolini's regime had not (yet) introduced its own race laws, Mussolini had been prepared to use an anti-semitic dog whistle on numerous occasions in his climb to political power; as well as drawing on the concept of "racial hygiene". In a November 1919 speech to Parliament he stated: *"I mean to say that Fascism has to deal with the race problem. The Fascists have to take care of the*

---

[34] Mussolini quoted in Ivo Herzer, pp 36-37

health of the race that will make history." In part, Mussolini was able to reject "biological" racism because of an alternative "cultural" and "spiritual" theory of racism that was influential in Italy of the time.

These developments in Italy were unfolding as Primo Levi was growing to adulthood. Like other Italian children he was taught Dante's *Inferno*. Yet there is a place so deep in hell that Virgil could not bear to show it to Dante. Science, in unholy coupling with prejudice, indifference and self-interest, raised it into the living world in our own times: and called it Auschwitz. Primo passed through that hell, and survived. Although, until Fascism made of him a thing to be exterminated, Levi hadn't given any importance to his Jewishness.

In a short story he wrote decades later, *Zinc*, Levi tells us of his life as a young chemistry student. Like countless young men before him he meets a girl: Rita. And he shares the exhilaration of his first faltering steps of getting to know her. It could be the story of any young couple, except, as his world begins to tell him, he is different.

But for now, he is just a chemistry student and his crises and victories are those of the first day of a new lab, where his task is to work with Zinc: a "boring" and "colourless" metal. The task is simple: combine zinc with diluted sulfuric acid. But Zinc has a strange property. When it is pure, it refuses to combine with other chemicals. The slightly impure kind is needed to make it useful. To Levi, purity was something disgustingly moralistic. Impurity, however, was the stuff of life itself.

> *"In order for the wheel of life to turn, for life to be lived, impurities are needed ... because I too am Jewish, and she is not: I am the impurity that makes the zinc react ..."*[35]

It was during that month that the madness of racism tightened its grip on Italy. In that month, Primo came to know that he was to be considered an impurity. Something that had been of little importance to him at a personal level now marked out a path. A path that step by step would drag him to Auschwitz.

In July and August of 1938, a racial manifesto was published in Italian newspapers. This manifesto claimed that races were biologically "real" (something science has now categorically refuted). But the manifesto was not done. It claimed that Italians were a "pure race" and that the "ancient purity of Italian blood" was "the greatest title of nobility of the Italian Nation". Italy's Jews were a particular target of the manifesto. It claimed:

> *"The Jews do not belong to the Italian race ... The Jews represent the sole population that has never assimilated itself in Italy because it is constituted of non-European racial elements, absolutely different to those of Italian origin."*[36]

---

[35] Primo Levi, pp 34-35
[36] The Defence of the Race, July 1938

The vacuity of the manifesto self-evident, if we recall that it was only a handful of decades since Italy had existed as a country at all. At the time, one of the Risorgimento politicians, Massimo d'Azeglio had famously stated: *"Now that we have made Italy, we must make Italians."*

With sleight of hand, an invented people had become an eternal pure substance. Scientific nonsense became dogma and lies became truth. This new dogma, moreover, was to be taught to children from their earliest years.

This manifesto was signed, not by the uneducated, the *anafabeti* of Italy, as they were long called; but by the learned. Holders of high academic and scientific office. Ten among Italy's learned men of medicine, anthropology, neuropsychiatry, paediatrics, endocrinology, zoology, demography and physiology and biology signed.

With the canonization of this new orthodoxy, worse followed quickly. Doctrine became steel-hard laws. In September 1938, these laws authorised the expulsion of Jewish teachers and children of Jewish background from schools. A systematic program of legal persecution was beginning to affect every part of life. Quickly systematic persecution, discrimination and exclusion were implemented. In all walks of life, Jews were to be expelled. Military service, business, owning land, membership of political parties, administrative service, local councils, banks, insurance work, universities and cultural academies were all closed to Italian Jews. Non-Italian Jews were to be expelled from the country. Libraries were to be "purified" of "Jewish" content.

Primo had entered university before the new laws and was allowed to finish his degree, but he struggled to find a supervisor. His university degree was marked with the words "Of Jewish race". With the help of friends, he found work as a chemist, using false papers.

Meanwhile, the allies landed on the Italian mainland in September 1943. In bitter fighting they began their slow advance along the Italian peninsula. After entering an armistice with the allies, the Italian government had fallen and been replaced by the Germans with a new puppet regime, with Mussolini reinstalled at its head. It continued to hold out in northern Italy. Where the regime persisted, Italy's Jews were behind "enemy lines".

And as the war ground on, the maws of hell opened. The Germans had already begun to send Italian Jews to the death camps, when, on 30 November 1943, Mussolini's remnant regime, signed *"Police Order No. 5"* into law. In a macabre competition with the Nazi regime, it was Italy's own mandate for the rounding up and deportation of Italy's Jews for extermination in Germany's death camps.[37]

In the hell it created for Primo, there was no "castle of the

---

[37] See Joshua Zimmerman and Shira Klein

learned" like the one we find in Dante's Limbo. The learned who fashioned this hell for their fellow human beings did not descend into it. It was a hell in which human ashes were spread to make paths for those who yet living.

Primo Levi's greatest contribution to human rights was to unveil the reality of the depravity that the Holocaust represented. His book *If this is a Man,* is one of the most important Holocaust narratives. It is recognised as a great work of Italian literature. Together with *The Truce*, which tells of his return to Italy, it became a standard text in Italian schools. During his life, Levi visited over 130 schools speaking of his experiences.

The war through which Primo Levi had lived was more horrific than the world had ever seen. It had slaughtered millions, turned cities to ash and, among its worst manifestations, had made laboratory animals of human beings. For the survivors who were charged with rebuilding the world anew there was a short window of time before mutually suspicious allies became enemies. A short time for the lessons of the war to be embodied in a new path. That path was the Universal Declaration of Human Rights. Eleanor Roosevelt was to play a central role in ensuring that path came into being.

CHAPTER EIGHT
Eleanor Roosevelt

"Everyone has duties to the community in which alone the free and full development of his personality is possible."

1948 UNIVERSAL DECLARATION OF HUMAN RIGHTS,
ARTICLE 29(1)

Eleanor Roosevelt was the first Chair of the United Nations Human Rights Commission. Her work, with her colleagues, led to the adoption in 1948 of the Universal Declaration of Human Rights.

Yet, she was a remarkable woman long before she was given the role of chair of the Human Rights Commission. Among other things, she was recognised for her work for the poor and was a frequent advocate of the rights of African Americans of her own country.

In 1939, the Daughters of the American Revolution, of which she was a member, refused to let Marian Anderson, an African American singer, perform in Constitution Hall. Eleanor Roosevelt not only resigned her membership, she organised a free open-air concert for Anderson at the Lincoln Memorial, drawing an audience of 75,000 people. It was her role as an advocate of equal rights, as much as her standing as a former First Lady of the United States, that led to her election as first chairperson of the UN Commission on Human Rights.

On the tenth anniversary of the Declaration, she spoke of the importance of human rights being realised "close to home":

> *Where, after all, do universal human rights begin? In small places, close to home — so close and so small that they cannot be seen on any map of the world. Yet they are the world of the individual person: the neighborhood he lives in; the school or college he attends; the factory, farm or office where he works. Such are the places where every man, woman, and child seeks equal justice, equal opportunity, equal dignity without discrimination. Unless these rights have meaning there, they have little meaning anywhere. Without concerted citizen action to*

uphold them close to home, we shall look in vain for progress in the larger world.[38]

The drafting committee appointed by the Commission on Human Rights were the Commission Chair, Eleanor Roosevelt, Peng Chun Chang, its Vice Chair (who among other things contributed Confucian ideas to the drafting) and Charles Malik, the Rapporteur.

They first met in June 1947, and John Humphrey attended on behalf of the UN Secretariat. He was a Canadian law professor and the first head of the UN Division of Human Rights. He, together with staff of the UN Secretariat, prepared the first draft of the Declaration.

Other members were later added to the drafting committee, including Rene Cassin of France (who had lost most of his family in the Holocaust and who produced the second draft of the Declaration) and Hansa Mehta of India, who strongly advocated for language which was inclusive of the rights and equality of women.

The Universal Declaration was not drafted in a vacuum, rather its ideas were drawn from existing human rights instruments and ideas from around the world. There was a rich heritage from which the Declaration was crystallised. Some of that heritage has been explored in these pages. The list of rights which appears in the early

---

[38] These words delivered at the launch of a campaign kit for the Universal Declaration titled "In Your Hands: A Guide for Community Action", is widely reproduced.

drafts largely survived through to the final version of the Declaration. However, two statements that John Humphrey had included in the first draft did not survive into the final version. They were along the following lines.

1. *We are citizens both of our countries and of the world.*

2. *There can be no human freedom or dignity unless war and the threat of war is abolished.*

Without Eleanor Roosevelt, the Declaration may never have been concluded at all. Knowing her own country, the United States, was not ready to accept a binding treaty, she urged that a Declaration be pursued instead. At the time the United States was arguably the most powerful country in the world. The result was a document, which like the US Declaration of Independence, although not legally binding, has been and remains profoundly influential. Ever since its adoption it has shaped the values of the United Nations and the world community. As Eleanor Roosevelt saw, a treaty, even though binding, would in many ways have been weaker.

In time, the binding law emerged on the foundations that the Declaration had laid. Not just one treaty, but a whole family of treaties each protecting a different dimension of human rights.

Charles Malik succeeded Eleanor Roosevelt as chair of the Commission. On 6 November 1948 he introduced the

Universal Declaration of Human Rights, newly completed, to the Third Committee of the UN General Assembly. Here are some of his words that day.

> "... the phrase human rights and fundamental freedoms is mentioned seven times in the charter of the world organization, but nowhere is it precisely defined. Just what are my basic rights and my irreducible freedoms? ... this question is not answered. What we are trying to do in the Declaration ... is enumerate in precise terms ... fundamental rights and freedoms. Thus, we state that you and I are born free and equal. That we are endowed with reason and conscience. That there should be no discrimination between men and women of all sorts and kinds. That no one shall be held in slavery or servitude. That no one shall be subjected to arbitrary arrest.
>
> We declare the right of asylum and the right of nationality. We declare the right of property and the right of marriage, the right to freedom of thought, freedom of conscience and freedom of religion. We declare the right of freedom of assembly and association, the right to social security, to a decent standard of living, to education and leisure and to the enjoyment of art and scientific advancement.
>
> The important thing in all this, is that the Declaration will be the outcome of the combined thought of fifty-eight nations. It will therefore express the fundamental convictions of the present age with respect to what constitutes the dignity of man. It will be an

international document of the first order of importance. And it will be read and pondered by our children's children."[39]

When the Declaration was finally adopted on 10 December 1948, Eleanor Roosevelt was able to announce as a delegate of the United States that her country would give the declaration its full support.

According to her son, Eleanor Roosevelt, would every night finish her day with the following prayer:

"Our Father, who has set a restlessness in our hearts and made us all seekers after that which we can never fully find, forbid us to be satisfied with what we make of life.

"Draw us from base content and set our eyes on far off goals. Keep us at tasks too hard for us that we may be driven to Thee for strength.

"Deliver us from fretfulness and self-pitying; make us sure of the good we cannot see and of the hidden good in the world.

"Open our eyes to simple beauty all around us and our hearts to the loveliness men hide from us because we do not try to understand them.

"Save us from ourselves and show us a vision of the world made new."[40]

---

[39] Charles Malik, 6 November 1948
[40] Cited by Mary Ann Glendon

The last line of the prayer inspired the title of Mary Ann Glendon's book *A World Made New – Eleanor Roosevelt and the Universal Declaration of Human Rights*. Eleanor Roosevelt's prayer appears in the frontispiece of the book which tells the story of how the Universal Declaration of Human Rights was written and the contribution that Eleanor Roosevelt made to that process. Although she was not directly engaged in writing the declaration, as Chair of the UN Human Rights Commission, Eleanor Roosevelt's leadership ensured the Commission succeeded in its work.

On the Tenth Anniversary a kit for community action was launched which promoted the Universal Declaration of Human Rights as a focus for advocacy in the United States. Much of the concern of the booklet was on the questions of segregation and discrimination which was still widespread in the country (despite being outlawed in many individual states). The civil rights movement would soon take the ideas of the Declaration from the halls of the United Nations to the streets of the United States. Martin Luther King Jr. was a central figure in what happened next.

CHAPTER NINE
Martin Luther King Jr.

"... any doctrine of racial differentiation or superiority is scientifically false, morally condemnable, socially unjust and dangerous, and ... there is no justification for racial discrimination either in theory or in practice, ..."

1963 UNITED NATIONS DECLARATION ON THE
ELIMINATION OF ALL FORMS OF RACIAL DISCRIMINATION, PREAMBLE

The Reverend Dr. Martin Luther King Jr. lived a life beyond the ordinary. While this chapter will not do justice to his life, we will seek to learn what Martin Luther King Jr.'s life teaches us about human rights and their meaning. We will focus on Martin Luther King's thought, mainly as expressed in his recorded speeches and his own life. Of course, he was part of a broader movement which had many thousands of significant contributors as well as millions of supporters.

In popular media, Martin Luther King Jr. is understood almost exclusively as a leader of the civil rights movement. This of course he was, and it was central to his work. But the picture is incomplete. Other aspects of his thought include the spiritual reservoir from which he drew; his advocacy of nonviolent methods; his profound belief in the interconnectedness of all human beings; his advocacy of the rights of the poor generally; and his passionate appeals in the cause of peace. Words spoken by Coretta King on 6 April 1968, following her husband's assassination, captured important dimensions of his work.

> *"Martin Luther King, Jr. gave his life for the poor of the world, the garbage workers of Memphis and the peasants of Vietnam. The day that Negro people and others in bondage are truly free, on the day want is abolished, on the day wars are no more, on that day I know my husband will rest in a long-deserved peace."*[41]

He is a figure who stands at the birth of the world in which we now live. His life indeed represents a watershed between a world in which racism was still

---

[41] Henry Epps, p 284

normal and protected by the powers of state and law; and one in which racism was finally placed beyond the pale. In our world today, racism (if still not universally) is a condemned ideology. We are so used to this reality that we may unconsciously project our context back to the world as it was in his time. Over and over we hear Martin Luther King's words echoed in our popular media: "I have a dream". We enjoy the benefits of the translation of Martin Luther King's dream into reality.

As a civil rights leader, he worked for, and gave his life to end racial segregation and racism in the United States. His work was part of a global trajectory which has rejected the ideology of racism. While racism still exists in the world, while it is still virulent and hateful, while it still seeks to fasten on young minds, while so much remains to be done, and the struggle is far from over, racism is an ideology of the past, not the future.

Martin Luther King Jr's human rights work was deeply motivated by his personal history and commitment as a Christian leader. This source can be seen in how he conceived of the struggle to contribute to a more just world, and as a spiritual reservoir which gave strength and resilience to his work. His adoption of methods of nonviolence to pursue civil rights goals is an important aspect of what he did.

His advocacy of peace represents one of the main unfinished domains of the work which he left us. While we may be tempted to think of these dimensions as separate, it is likely that for him, they were part of a single integral whole. For example, his advocacy for peace built on his advocacy for human rights, and he explained it, a necessary extension of the work he did in the civil rights movement.

Martin Luther King Jr. lived from 1929 until his assassination on 4 April 1968, aged just thirty-nine. His death, along with the killings of John and Robert Kennedy in the space of a few years brought an end to a visionary era of progressive leadership in the United States.

Before looking further at his life and thought, a review of the changes associated with the Civil Rights Movement, give a sense of the scope of the transformation to which Martin Luther King contributed. The following are pieces of legislation designed to address the injustices that were among the fruits of the civil rights movement.

The Civil Rights Act of 1964 prohibited discrimination on the basis of race, colour or national origin in employment and public accommodation. The Voting Rights Act of 1965 protected the right of all citizens to vote. The Immigration and Nationality Services Act of 1965 opened immigration to the United States to non-Europeans and the Fair Housing Act of 1965 banned discrimination in the sale and rental of private housing.

Each item of legislation addressed a real and deep field of injustice, most of which were particularly experienced by

African Americans. Martin Luther King's words capture some of these profound denials, in ways that such a list cannot.

> *"Perhaps it is easy for those who have never felt the stinging darts of segregation to say, "Wait." But when you have seen vicious mobs lynch your mothers and fathers at will and drown your sisters and brothers at whim; when you have seen hate filled policemen curse, kick and even kill your black brothers and sisters; when you see the vast majority of your twenty million Negro brothers smothering in an airtight cage of poverty in the midst of an affluent society; when you suddenly find your tongue twisted and your speech stammering as you seek to explain to your six year old daughter why she can't go to the public amusement park that has just been advertised on television, and see tears welling up in her eyes when she is told that Funtown is closed to colored children, and see ominous clouds of inferiority beginning to form in her little mental sky, and see her beginning to distort her personality by developing an unconscious bitterness toward white people; when you have to concoct an answer for a five year old son who is asking: "Daddy, why do white people treat colored people so mean?"; when you take a cross county drive and find it necessary to sleep night after night in the uncomfortable corners of your automobile because no motel will accept you; when you are humiliated day in and day out by nagging signs reading "white" and*

"colored"; when your first name becomes "nigger," your middle name becomes "boy" (however old you are) and your last name becomes "John," and your wife and mother are never given the respected title "Mrs."; when you are harried by day and haunted by night by the fact that you are a Negro, living constantly at tiptoe stance, never quite knowing what to expect next, and are plagued with inner fears and outer resentments; when you are forever fighting a degenerating sense of "nobodiness"–then you will understand why we find it difficult to wait."[42]

The oppression the civil rights movement addressed was as pervasive and profound as any in human history.

As a civil rights leader, Martin Luther's achievement is of course captured in his "I have a dream" speech of 28 August 1968. It is so well-known that it hardly needs repetition. As a speaker he was masterful, but that mastery was not only in respect of words, it was in respect of ideas. He framed the civil rights movement as a universal movement for the fulfilment *of the accepted but unrealised* values of the society to which he belonged. In doing so, he enabled those around him to see and conceive of the civil rights movement not as an African American movement solely concerned with African American rights – but rather as a universal movement concerned with the realisation of deeply shared human

---

[42] Martin Luther King Jr., Letter from a Birmingham Jail

values and aspirations. In its fullest sense his vision of justice included all human beings.

What role did Christianity play in Martin Luther King Jr's civil rights advocacy?

Martin Luther King Jr. was born in Atlanta Georgia, the second son of Martin Luther King Sr. and Alberta Williams King.

Martin Luther King Jr. was by vocation a Baptist minister. He was in the fourth generation of his family to take up this vocation. It is impossible to fully appreciate Martin Luther King's work without understanding the role that Christian thought and inspiration played in his advocacy of human rights.

Martin Luther King's letter from a Birmingham prison to fellow Christian clergy gives insight on the role his religious commitment played in generating and sustaining his commitment to work for justice. Further, the people from whom he came, the African Americans who struggled against centuries of slavery and racism, drew from deep spiritual and human reservoirs in the long and bitter journey from slavery, through oppression and segregation, before the civil rights reforms were won.

In setting out why he was in Birmingham he explicitly drew on a 'prophetic role'.

> *"I am in Birmingham because injustice is here. Just as the prophets of the eight century B.C. left their villages*

and carried their "thus saith the Lord" far beyond the boundaries of their home towns ... so I am compelled to carry the gospel of freedom beyond my home town."[43]

In explaining the nonviolent methods he practised, which were criticised by his fellow clergy and to whom he was responding, he wrote:

"We have waited more than 340 years for our constitutional and God-given rights."[44]

He drew on biblical precedents for civil disobedience to the law, "on the ground that a higher moral law was at stake". Human rights, as he conceived them, do not depend on the decision of any human agency. As a consequence, they can never be overridden by any human decision. It is a perspective which in the final analysis places human rights beyond the reach of any tyrant, no matter how powerful, and beyond the reach of any rationalisation offered by the powerful that claims a justification for the oppression of human beings.

In thinking about Martin Luther King's Christianity, we would again miss something significant to his human rights advocacy if we didn't consider how his spiritual practice was engaged in that work. The role that prayer played in Martin Luther King's work, is captured in a recollection from his wife Coretta King.

---

[43] Martin Luther King Jr., Letter from a Birmingham Jail
[44] Martin Luther King Jr., Letter from a Birmingham Jail

"Prayer was a wellspring of strength and inspiration during the Civil Rights Movement. Throughout the movement, we prayed for greater human understanding. We prayed for the safety of our compatriots in the freedom struggle. We prayed for victory in our nonviolent protests, for brotherhood and sisterhood among people of all races, for reconciliation and the fulfillment of the Beloved Community.

For my husband, Martin Luther King, Jr. prayer was a daily source of courage and strength that gave him the ability to carry on in even the darkest hours of our struggle.

"After the call, he got up from bed and made himself some coffee. He began to worry about his family, and all of the burdens that came with our movement weighed heavily on his soul. With his head in his hands, Martin bowed over the kitchen table and prayed aloud to God: "Lord, I am taking a stand for what I believe is right. The people are looking to me for leadership, and if I stand before them without strength and courage, they will falter. I am at the end of my powers. I have nothing left. I have nothing left. I have come to the point where I can't face it alone."

"I remember one very difficult day when he came home bone-weary from the stress that came with his leadership of the Montgomery Bus Boycott. In the middle of that night, he was awakened by a threatening and abusive phone call, one of many we received throughout the

movement. On this particular occasion, however, Martin had had enough.

"Later he told me, "At that moment, I experienced the presence of the Divine as I had never experienced Him before. It seemed as though I could hear a voice saying: 'Stand up for righteousness; stand up for truth; and God will be at our side forever.'" When Martin stood up from the table, he was imbued with a new sense of confidence, and he was ready to face anything."[45]

If one happens not to share Martin Luther King's faith, what meaning can be drawn from what is described here? Within the act of prayer, part of what is described is Martin Luther King's search for and discovery of knowledge in a time of deep uncertainty.

In the next chapter we will look at the life of Justice Albie Sachs. Justice Sachs describes himself as Jewish but non-religious: "not practising in any way". Yet he states in his book:

"I did in fact have a strong set of beliefs, my own world view, in many ways a deeply spiritual one with overwhelming ethical implications."[46]

Speaking of solving problems in the law, he speaks about moments of inspiration as being the most creative and productive:

---

[45] Schomberg Centre for Research in Black Culture, pp x-xi
[46] Albie Sachs, p 235

> *"only when I had been close to being in what my Buddhist friends would call a transcendental meditational state, would these formulations emerge, as if from nowhere ... it so happened that the first three times I was cited in foreign jurisdictions, the formulations had all come to me at moments when my brain had been least engaged in hard legal reasoning."*[47]

Looked at in ways that transcend mere words, there is much that is common in the human experience. The inner resources that Martin Luther King drew upon do not depend on how we choose to describe ourselves nor on the particular model of reality we may hold. They likely do depend on some form of engagement with our inner "spiritual" life; however we might describe or understand it.

Most poignantly, the deep spirituality of Martin Luther King's journey, is captured in the final words of the speech he delivered the evening before his murder. There were fears that evening. Threats had been made. He spoke of how happy he was to live in the time of the civil rights movement, having survived an earlier assassination attempt, and having seen the victories that had been won. How happy he was to have lived long enough to undertake the work he felt he had to do, and had now completed. In his last words he was a Moses to his people.

---

[47] Albie Sachs, p 117

"Well, I don't know what will happen to me now. We've got some difficult days ahead. But it doesn't matter what happens to me now. Because I've been to the mountaintop. And I don't mind. Like anybody, I would like to live a long life. Longevity has its place. But I'm not concerned about that now. I just want to do God's will. And He's allowed me to go up to the mountain. And I've looked over. And I've seen the promised land. I may not get there with you. But I want you to know tonight that we, as a people will get to the promised land. And I'm happy tonight. I'm not worried about anything. I'm not fearing any man. Mine eyes have seen the glory of the coming of the Lord."[48]

The spiritual roots of human rights on which he drew, are also seen in his speech titled "the American Dream", delivered in 1964, where he spoke on the concept of rights, as found in the U.S. Declaration of Independence. He describes its well-known opening phrases affirming the core values of human rights as "a dream." He means it is a dream that neither existed at the time the Declaration was originally written, nor did it exist in his own day. He identifies as distinctive of this dream that:

"It says that each individual has certain basic rights that are neither derived from nor conferred by the state. They are gifts from the hands of the Almighty God."[49]

---

[48] Martin Luther King Jr., I've Been to the Mountaintop
[49] Martin Luther King Jr., The American Dream (1965)

In his speech in 1964 accepting the Nobel Peace Prize his words speak of the power of "faith". In this case his words are not so much addressing "religious" faith, as addressing a "faith" that sustains the struggle against oppression, even in the direst circumstances.

> *"I refuse to accept the view that mankind is so tragically bound to the starless midnight of racism and war that the bright daybreak of peace and brotherhood can never become a reality. ...*
>
> *"I still believe that mankind will bow before the altars of God and be crowned triumphant over war and bloodshed ... I still believe that we shall overcome.*
>
> *"This faith can give us courage to face the uncertainties of the future. It will give our tired feet new strength as we continue our forward stride toward the city of freedom. When our days become dreary with low-hovering clouds and our nights become darker than a thousand midnights, we will know that we are living in the creative turmoil of a genuine civilization struggling to be born."*[50]

These are the words of a man and a people whose faith have sustained them through centuries of oppression.

In international fora, and in the 21st century, human rights work is generally carried on without reference to any 'higher authority'.

---

[50] Martin Luther King, Acceptance Speech Nobel Peace Prize 1964

In part, this is a consequence of the need for universality – the necessity of adopting and speaking in a language and concepts that are accessible for all human beings irrespective of historical background and irrespective of belief. In other words, the importance of using language that does not exclude the dreams of any human being for justice. Thus when, in 1948, the Universal Declaration of Human Rights re-expressed "the dream", it did not mention "God". Not because faith was not important to a number of those involved in the creation of the Declaration, (it was), but because those involved felt this new language should be a wider dream inclusive of all human beings irrespective of "belief".

Their insight was of course right.

However, a heavy price is paid if, from a justifiable concern for universality, we disconnect human rights from its genuine human history.

One price is the unmooring of human rights from the lives of the human beings whose struggles took "the dream" of human rights and made it manifest in the physical world. Many, as a matter of historical fact, were motivated by their religious beliefs. Many were not. But human rights cannot be understood if the actual stories of the human beings involved are not told and re-told.

Further if we do not tell the real history, other narratives are substituted that impoverish human rights history. Paul Gilroy in his oration *Race and the Right to be Human* has captured this well, and his insights are quoted in the introduction to this book.

Needless to say, the substitute history that has arisen is deeply inaccurate and does a disservice to the cause of human rights. Most importantly, in words that Martin Luther King Jr. might use, the *"ought"* of human rights is displaced and substituted by the *"is"* of the now. This "now" was, in Martin Luther King's time, and remains in our own, in many ways profoundly unjust.

Waves of human rights violations continue to crash before the bastion of human indifference and self-interest. To let an unjust present appropriate and clothe itself in human rights, places a high and unjustified barrier in the way further human rights progress. It disempowers those who like Martin Luther King, seek a better future than today.

Thirdly, there is a specific methodology which human rights forebears like Martin Luther King employed in the cause of human rights. This methodology is also lost when human rights are unmoored from its history. Gilroy refers to this aspect as "sentimentality". The language of human rights, at its most effective, speaks to both heart and mind, as Martin Luther King did. Others well before him also did the same, as Paul Gilroy also notes, giving the example of Angelina Grimké who in 1838 wrote to her friend Catherine Beecher:

"The investigation of the rights of the slave has led me to

> *better understanding of our own. I have found the Antislavery cause to be the high school of morals in our land — the school in which human rights are more fully investigated and better understood and taught, than in any other. Here a great fundamental principle is uplifted and illuminated, and from this central light rays innumerable stream all around. Human beings have rights, because they are moral beings: the rights of all men grown out of their moral nature, they have essentially the same rights."*[51]

The exclusion of such aspects of human rights creates a vacuum which is filled with an imagined and disconnected reality.

That imagined reality sometimes has the character of a dry and soulless legalism that reduces the great principles and values of human rights to mere rules to be forensically applied to determine a legal outcome. They implicitly substitute treaty rules and legal regulation for true humanity and a true spirit of "brotherhood". As we saw above, Martin Luther King was well aware that human rights do not come from documents: *"they are neither conferred by nor derive from the state"*.

Gandhi perhaps captured this well when responding to a letter from UNESCO asking for input towards the drafting of the Universal Declaration of Human Rights. The substance of his reply is brief:

---

[51] Cited by Paul Gilroy

"I'm afraid I can't give you anything approaching your minimum. That I have no time for the effort is true enough. But what is truer is that I am a poor reader of literature past or present much as I should like to read some of its gems. Living a stormy life since my early youth, I had no leisure to do the necessary reading.

"I learnt from my illiterate but wise mother that all rights to be deserved and preserved come from duty well done. Thus the very right to live accrues to us only when we do the duty of citizenship of the world. From this one fundamental statement, perhaps it is easy enough to define the duties of Man and Woman and correlate every right to some corresponding duty to be first performed. Every other right can be shown to be an usurpation hardly worth fighting for."[52]

Indirectly, Gandhi expresses a source of human rights which is far deeper than any documentary, or even philosophical source. He communicates a life of struggle that billions have faced over history, and continue to face today: a life in which there is no leisure to read. It is from these human beings that the universal cry for justice has echoed through history. He also expresses human rights in terms that anyone in the human rights movement will understand as lived experience. Human rights are not achieved without taking up the duty to contribute to their realisation.

---

[52] Mahatma Gandhi, 1947, p 3

There are numerous insights we can draw from the spiritual foundations of Martin Luther King's work, irrespective of our own beliefs. Not only does each of us have human rights, we owe them to no human institution. We possess human rights "inherently" in our humanity. The struggle for a more just world is a shared struggle and we have a right and obligation to stand for others human rights, just as much as our own. Human rights are as much a characteristic of the human heart as the human mind. As much as laws may assist in the realisation of human rights; they are an inadequate repository for them. The struggle for human rights requires faith in our ability as human beings to create a more just order. It requires us to draw on our inner 'spiritual' reserve. No matter how dark the immediate horizon may be; no matter how far the dawn; the hour will come when the oppressions of today are no more.

There is something else. In a world that is in our own day so publicly secular and distrustful of the contribution that religion might make; something is surprising. We have largely forgotten how recently it was that Christians of deep faith played a pivotal role in one of the key human rights struggles of history.

Martin Luther King Jr. and Non-violence

Martin Luther King Jr. thought deeply about the best methods to use to overcome the injustices facing African Americans. This in itself is an important observation. At its core is the importance of asking questions about whether proposed methods are both ethical and effective given a human rights issue to be addressed.

His speeches frequently describe and defend nonviolence as the method he felt was both effective and moral for the issues on which he worked. Sometimes the description was in response to criticism of the method as "too extreme", at other times it was to reject the violence advocated by others.

His explanations were patient and detailed.

The basic steps of the method are outlined to his fellow ministers in his letter from a Birmingham jail.

> *"In any nonviolent campaign there are four basic steps: collection of the facts to determine whether injustices exist; negotiation; self-purification; and direct action. We have gone through all these steps in Birmingham."*[53]

In his American dream speech, he identifies three characteristics of the method: its effectiveness, its moral grounding and its characteristic of love.

> *"First I should say that I am still convinced that the most potent weapon available to oppressed people in their struggle for freedom and human dignity is nonviolent resistance. I am convinced that this is a powerful method. It disarms the opponent, it exposes his moral defences, it weakens his morale and at the same time it works on his*

---

[53] Martin Luther King Jr., Letter from a Birmingham Jail

conscience, and he just doesn't know how to deal with it. ... If he beats you, you develop the courage of accepting blows without retaliating ... if he puts you in jail, you go in that jail and transform it from a dungeon of shame to a haven of freedom and human dignity ..."[54]

In regard to its morality, he makes observations such as the following.

"[nonviolence] makes it possible for individuals to struggle to secure moral ends through moral means ... because in a real sense the end is pre-existent in the means. And the means represent the ideal in the making and the end in the process."[55]

As to love he explains:

"It says it is possible to struggle passionately and unrelentingly against an unjust system and yet not stoop to hatred in the process. The love ethic can stand at the centre of a nonviolent movement."[56]

He draws on his training in classical Greek which has three words for different kinds of love, to explain how it is possible, not to like, but to love an oppressor. He is not speaking of *"eros"* (aesthetic or romantic love) or *"philia"* (love grounded in friendship). Rather he means *"agape"*.

"Agape is understanding, creative redemptive good will

---

[54] Martin Luther King Jr., Independence Day
[55] Martin Luther King Jr., Independence Day
[56] Martin Luther King, The American Dream (1964)

> *for all men. It is an overflowing love that seeks nothing in return. Theologians would say that it is the love of God operating in the human heart. And when one rises to love on this level, he loves every man, not because he likes him but because God loves him. And he rises to the level of loving the person who does the evil deed while hating the deed that the person does. And this I think is the kind of love that can guide us through the days and weeks and years ahead. This is the kind of love that can help us achieve and create the beloved community"*[57]

These three underlying rationales of the method can be applied to consider questions of human rights methodology in any struggle. Will the proposed advocacy be effective (produce good rather than harm)? Is it moral? Is it grounded in universal love for humankind?

A further dimension of the nonviolent approach taught by Martin Luther King was that the inspiration was derived from Gandhi's nonviolent movement for self-determination against British colonialism. In his American Dream speech Martin Luther King says, *"we will meet your physical force with soul force."* In the Gandhian original 'soul force' is *'satyagraha'*. We often equate "power" with physical force. Here he is drawing our attention to immaterial forms of "power", which

---

[57] Martin Luther King Jr., Loving Your Enemies; Martin Luther King Jr., Independence Day

have nothing to do with violence, and indeed have no need of it.

In his speech on accepting the Nobel Peace Prize, Martin Luther King states explicitly the source of the nonviolent method:

> "Negroes of the United States, following the people of India, have demonstrated that nonviolence is not sterile passivity, but a powerful moral force which makes for moral transformation."[58]

In his 1959 article "My trip to the land of Gandhi" he expands further:

> "While the Montgomery boycott was going on, India's Gandhi was the guiding light of our technique of non-violent social change. We spoke of him often … I was delighted that the Gandhians accepted us with open arms. They praised our experiment with the non-violent resistance technique at Montgomery. They seem to look upon it as an outstanding example of the possibilities of its use in western civilization."[59]

What is striking about the Gandhian connection is that, although drawing from completely different philosophical traditions, people facing oppressions a world apart, discovered common principles, values and methods for the attainment of human rights. This is the

---

[58] Martin Luther King Jr., Acceptance Speech Nobel Peace Prize 1964
[59] Martin Luther King Jr., My Trip to the Land of Gandhi

universality of human rights.

It is clear that Martin Luther King saw nonviolence as a method of addressing oppression and violence that is worthy of human dignity.

> *"... nonviolence is the answer to the crucial political and moral question of our time – the need for man to overcome oppression and violence without resorting to violence and oppression. Civilization and violence are antithetical concepts. ... man must evolve for all human conflict a method which rejects revenge, aggression and retaliation. The foundation of such a method is love."*[60]

Although proven to be more effective and of course more moral than violent methods, nonviolent methods of overcoming oppression have been attempted in recent decades with mixed results. In Eastern Europe they were often successful in ending totalitarian regimes and establishing inclusive governance that better serves the needs of the people. The Philippines offers another example of effective nonviolent change.

In a number of cases attempts at nonviolent change were followed by an outbreak of violence that dragged society into profoundly worse conditions. Among recent examples are Libya, Syria, Egypt, and conflicts in Eastern Europe.

Nonviolence is not always effective. The factors that came

---

[60] Martin Luther King Jr., Acceptance Speech Nobel Peace Prize 1964

together for success in the U.S. civil rights movement are not always present. Yet violence and human rights are antithetical. Indeed, a purpose of human rights is to prevent violence, as affirmed in the preamble to the Universal Declaration of Human Rights.

Finally, in the early 21st century violence, even by a handful of individuals, has the power to destroy thousands of human lives, or to polarize and destabilize entire countries.

A question that we must seriously consider in the context of the increasingly easy and obscene resort to violence in the 21st century, is: are there even better methods than nonviolence? That is, are there methods which do not carry the risk of descent into a spiral of violence, or the risk of contributing to a polarisation which leads to civil conflict, or the risk of empowering new violence prone oppressors?

In the South African case, the end of apartheid seems to have been at least in part mediated by a process of negotiation and pursuit of shared goals by community leaders on both sides of the racial divide. In that case, the heirs of an unjust system were active participants in its dismantlement. This was of course also true of the civil rights reforms in the United States, which depended on support from federal authorities.

It may be observed that the nonviolent method can be seen as a dramatisation. It casts the people and communities involved in archetypal "evil" and "good" roles. For example, these words of Martin Luther King illuminate the method:

> *"Nonviolent direct action seeks to create such a crisis and foster such a tension that a community which has constantly refused to negotiate is forced to confront the issue. It seeks so to dramatize the issue that it can no longer be ignored. ...*
>
> *"Like a boil that can never be cured so long as it is covered up but must be opened with all its ugliness to the natural medicines of air and light, injustice must be exposed, with all the tension its exposure creates, to the light of human conscience and the air of national opinion before it can be cured."*[61]

An aspect of Martin Luther King's approach that perhaps was critical in achieving a successful outcome, was that his approach was not limited to making visible the evil of segregation; he also made visible a vision of a more enlightened community – 'the dream' – of which he often speaks. He led people towards that dream, as much as away from racism and segregation. In the end it was the vision unrealised, and the hope of its realisation that mobilised a movement.

What are the best methods for addressing the injustices and maladies of the 21st century? There is no easy answer

---

[61] Martin Luther King Jr., Letter from a Birmingham Jail

to this question. There are however other movements that perhaps provide insights that could be drawn on to greater extent in the human rights movement: the women's movement (for which no single bullet was ever fired); and the peace movement among them. Martin Luther King Jr., who thought long and carefully about questions of method, teaches us that such thought is required if human rights are to be successfully pursued in a manner worthy of human dignity. We should at least aspire to no less enlightened methods than the ones he pursued. And to all those who use or justify violence in our century in the name of "justice", Martin Luther King's life stands in reproach. If violence was not necessary to overcome 340 years of oppression; it is not necessary for any cause.

Something else that Martin Luther King observes in relation to nonviolence remains an important contribution of his thought – that the method of nonviolence transcends sectional interests and rejects the substitution of future tyrannies:

> "And he will realize that a doctrine of black supremacy is as dangerous as a doctrine of white supremacy, and that God is not interested merely in the freedom of black men, and brown men, and yellow men; but God is interested in the freedom of the whole human race and the creation of a society where all men will live together as brothers, and every man will respect the dignity and

worth of human personality."[62]

Martin Luther King, Peace and World Brotherhood

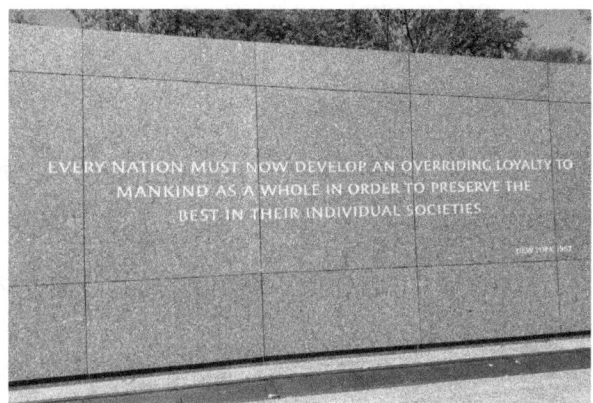

To fully appreciate Martin Luther King's thoughts on peace, we must understand his thoughts about the relationship between human beings.

He saw all human beings as caught *"in an inescapable network of mutuality, tied in a single garment of destiny."*[63] This thought unfolded in his February 1964 speech, "The American Dream".

> *"All I'm saying is simply this, that all life is interrelated. And we are caught in an inescapable network of mutuality, tied in a single garment of destiny — whatever affects one directly, affects all indirectly. For some strange reason I can never be what I ought to be*

---

[62] Martin Luther King Jr., SMU Speech 1966

[63] Martin Luther King Jr., Letter from a Birmingham Jail

until you are what you ought to be, and you can never be what you ought to be until I am what I ought to be. This is the interrelated structure of reality. ... I think this is the first challenge and it is necessary to meet it in order to move on toward the realization of the American Dream, the dream of men of all races, creeds, national backgrounds, living together as brothers."[64]

In this context he recasts the American Dream as a universal dream.

"I would like to start on the world scale, so to speak, by saying if the American Dream is to be a reality we must develop a world perspective. It goes without saying that the world in which we live is geographically one, and now more than ever before we are challenged to make it one in terms of brotherhood. ... through our scientific genius we have made of this world a neighborhood, and now through our moral and ethical commitment, we must make of it a brotherhood. We must all learn to live together as brothers or we will all perish together as fools. This is the challenge of the hour. No individual can live alone, no nation can live alone. Somehow we are interdependent."[65]

The implications of these insights on the nature of human relationships led to his advocacy of peace in the context of the Vietnam War.

---

[64] Martin Luther King Jr., The American Dream (1964)
[65] Martin Luther King Jr., The American Dream (1964)

In April 1967 in a speech titled "Beyond Vietnam", he outlined the reasons why he felt he had to speak out on the war in Vietnam.

> *"Over the past two years, as I have moved to break the betrayal of my own silences and to speak from the burnings of my own heart, as I have called for radical departures from destruction of Vietnam, many persons have questioned me about the wisdom of my path."*[66]

He offered seven reasons for his opposition.

First was the adverse impact of warfare on his efforts to alleviate poverty of African Americans.

> *"There is at the outset a very obvious and almost facile connection between the war in Vietnam and the struggle I and others have been waging in America. A few years ago there was a shining moment in that struggle. It seemed as if there was a real promise of hope for the poor, both black and white, through the poverty program ... Then came the buildup in Vietnam, and I watched this program broken and eviscerated as if it were some idle political plaything on a society gone mad on war. And I knew that America would never invest the necessary funds or energies in rehabilitation of its poor so long as adventures like Vietnam continued ... So I was increasingly compelled to see the war as an enemy of the poor and to attack it as such."*[67]

---

[66] Martin Luther King Jr., Beyond Vietnam
[67] Martin Luther King Jr., Beyond Vietnam

Second was the direct harm of the war on the lives of African American young men and families.

> "... it became clear to me that the war was doing far more than devastating the hopes of the poor at home. It was sending their sons and their brothers and their husbands to fight and to die in extraordinarily high proportions ... We were taking the black young men ... and sending them eight thousand miles away to guarantee liberties in Southeast Asia which they had not found in southwest Georgia and East Harlem. So we have been repeatedly faced with the cruel irony of watching Negro and white boys on TV screens as they kill and die together for a nation that has been unable to seat them together in the same schools."

Third was the need to speak against violence as a solution to problems.

> "As I have walked among the desperate, rejected, and angry young men, I have told them that Molotov cocktails and rifles would not solve their problems. ... But they asked, and rightly so, "What about Vietnam?" They asked if our own nation wasn't using massive doses of violence to solve its problems, ... Their questions hit home, and I knew that I could never again raise my voice against the violence of the oppressed in the ghettos without having first spoken clearly to the greatest purveyor of violence in the world today: my own government."

Fourth was the American Dream, that any solution must realise that dream in larger proportions.

> *"In a way we were agreeing with Langston Hughes, that black bard from Harlem, who had written earlier:*
>
> *"O, yes, I say it plain,*
>
> *America never was America to me,*
>
> *And yet I swear this oath —*
>
> *America will be!"*
>
> *Now it should be incandescently clear that no one who has any concern for the integrity and life of America today can ignore the present war ... America's soul ... can never be saved so long as it destroys the hopes of men the world over. So it is that those of us who are yet determined that "America will be" are led down the path of protest and dissent, working for the health of our land."*

Sixth, he cites his commitment as a Christian minister, in addition to the charge laid on him by the Nobel Peace Prize.

> *"To me, the relationship of this ministry to the making of peace is so obvious that I sometimes marvel at those who ask me why I am speaking against the war ... Have they forgotten that my ministry is in obedience to the one who loved his enemies so fully that he died for them?"*

Finally, he cites the oneness of humanity, the theme of "brotherhood".

> "Beyond the calling of race or nation or creed is this vocation of sonship and brotherhood. Because I believe that the Father is deeply concerned, especially for His suffering and helpless and outcast children, I come tonight to speak for them. This I believe to be the privilege and the burden of all of us who deem ourselves bound by allegiances and loyalties which are broader and deeper than nationalism and which go beyond our nation's self-defined goals and positions. We are called to speak for the weak, for the voiceless, for the victims of our nation, for those it calls "enemy," for no document from human hands can make these humans any less our brothers."

Here his words, in respect of how we view our fellow human beings, recall words he wrote to his fellow Ministers from his prison cell in Birmingham.

Segregation, to use the terminology of the Jewish philosopher Martin Buber, substitutes an *"I-it"* relationship for an *"I-thou"* relationship. In other words, it turns people with whom we should have a relationship of mutuality and equality into things. It is slavery writ large.

Later in his speech he turns to the question of values, calling for a "revolution of values".

> "I am convinced ... we as a nation must undergo a radical revolution of values. We must rapidly begin the shift from a thing-oriented society to a person-oriented

society. When machines and computers, profit motives and property rights, are considered more important than people, the giant triplets of racism, extreme materialism, and militarism are incapable of being conquered."

He continues on poverty:

"A true revolution of values will soon look uneasily on the glaring contrast of poverty and wealth."

On war:

"A true revolution of values will lay hand on the world order and say of war, "This way of settling differences is not just."

Finally, the capstone of the revolution in values for which he calls is an expansion of loyalties from the particular to the universal:

"A genuine revolution of values means in the final analysis that our loyalties must become ecumenical rather than sectional. Every nation must now develop an overriding loyalty to mankind as a whole in order to preserve the best in their individual societies."

It is a reorientation to humanity as a whole as the highest value. It is not however a vague "emotional bosh" he means:

"This call for a worldwide fellowship that lifts neighborly concern beyond one's tribe, race, class, and nation is in reality a call for an all-embracing and unconditional love for all mankind. This oft

misunderstood, this oft misinterpreted concept, ... has now become an absolute necessity for the survival of man. When I speak of love I am not speaking of some sentimental and weak response. I'm not speaking of that force which is just emotional bosh. I am speaking of that force which all of the great religions have seen as the supreme unifying principle of life. ... We can no longer afford to worship the god of hate or bow before the altar of retaliation. The oceans of history are made turbulent by the ever-rising tides of hate."

It is notable that his advocacy of this broader and higher vision of values caused him to be sharply attacked. After his Beyond Vietnam Speech, allies in the Civil Rights Movement questioned his judgement and 168 newspapers across America attacked him.[68] Since then Cornel West has spoken of the "Santa Clausification" of Martin Luther King Jr., referring to a national amnesia of his broader message.[69]

It is impossible to separate Martin Luther King's advocacy of peace from the other aspects of his thought. They are part of the same cloth, understood from different perspectives. In his views on war, he still speaks primarily to the same audience: the "oppressed" who have come on the journey of civil rights, but the audience is now re-conceptualised as "privileged" members of a

---

[68] National Public Radio 2010

[69] Zaid Jilani,

society benefiting from wider global inequities. Here he thus speaks with the same self-critical voice that the earlier abolitionists used against the slave trade.

When we consider his words, we see that they are far more than rhetoric. They communicate the insights of a complex world-view. We see that his words have considerable courage. Of course, to oppose segregation itself took great courage. To speak out against the Vietnam War, when he did, was also an act of courage. To speak out for a wider loyalty to humanity as a whole was, and remains, an act of courage. It is evident that he saw these stances as necessary for the welfare of those he served, and the dispossessed in the world as a whole.

As a human rights advocate, he spoke for peace in a time of war. Almost half a century later the world remains beset with wars. The same concerns of the adverse impacts of war on the attainment of human rights in his time, remain pertinent. It is moreover hardly possible to separate the cause of peace from the cause of human rights. They are in reality, one and the same cause. For human rights workers, peace is a necessary precondition for progress in human rights. When fear and war seize the public mind, human rights are stalled for years or decades and often hard-won principles are torn to shreds. In the case of the abolition of the slave trade, the Napoleonic Wars delayed abolition for 20 years. In conditions of war human rights, far from progressing, disappear. Brutality reigns. Appallingly, in the 21st century, while borders, barbed wire and walls are erected with ever greater efficiency between people, the boundaries between war and peace have virtually broken down. This represents an existential threat to human rights and to the human welfare they seek to protect.

Finally, few seem to appreciate the importance of what Martin Luther King communicated when he spoke of "wider loyalties", the deeper "dream", the journey which is still incomplete. For reasons which are mystifying, the establishment of a world society based on 'love – agape' between human beings, is rarely considered a 'serious' contribution to public policy.

Few advocate the "revolution in values" which Martin Luther King espoused. It is difficult to find, in our halls of learning, those who view the brother and sisterhood of humankind as a serious and essential human project. Rarely do the words of our political leaders rise to such a noble orientation worthy of human dignity. Even in the advocacy of those who stand for and devote their lives to human rights, often the theme of 'brother/sisterhood' falls far behind in a contest in which equality and freedom are out in front, and brother/sisterhood are placed far down the list of priorities.

If human rights are to achieve its purpose in the world, this third theme of human rights must be recaptured. If Martin Luther King is right, it must be brought to the centre of human rights advocacy, with all that implies.

CHAPTER TEN
Albie Sachs

"The States Parties to the present Convention declare that apartheid is a crime against humanity and that inhuman acts resulting from ... similar policies and practices of racial segregation and discrimination ... are crimes violating the principles of international law ..."

1974 UNITED NATIONS CONVENTION ON THE SUPPRESSION AND PUNISHMENT OF THE CRIME OF APARTHEID, ARTICLE 1

As we have seen, the civil rights movement defeated racist segregation in one of its greatest strongholds, yet on the southern shores of another continent something very like it still persisted under a different name: apartheid. A young lawyer named Albie Sachs was part of the struggle against it. Later he was to become a judge of South Africa's Constitutional Court. We will explore his contribution to human rights primarily through his semi-autobiographical book, *The Strange Alchemy of Law and Life*.

The victims and perpetrators of human rights abuses whisper from the pages of this short book. They speak to us of their struggle to realize their own humanity and recognize the human being in each other.

For a judge *The Strange Alchemy of Law and Life* is an unusual book. But then Albie Sachs is an unusual judge.[70] A member of the African National Congress and a legal adviser to it, when it was still a revolutionary movement, Albie Sachs' life moves from barely surviving a state sponsored terrorist bombing, to which he lost an arm and an eye, to sitting on the Constitutional Court of South Africa.

It is the kind of life that prompts reflection, and Albie Sachs weaves both life reflections and judicial

---

[70] Albie Sachs Creative Commons image, Ram.eisenberg - own work, CC BY-SA 3.0, https://commons.wikimedia.org/w/index.php?curid=7463219

pronouncement into his book: bringing to life the human rights struggles of a country that was steeped in racism and racial theory but ultimately embraced a different future.

The book is written from the perspective of victory. The monster of apartheid has been slain. We can forget how profoundly immovable apartheid had seemed. As Albie Sachs writes:

> *"In what seemed to many to be the most inhospitable terrain for constitutional justice in the world, the most advanced ideas on human dignity, equality and freedom have robustly and I hope enduringly, taken root."*[71]

His book traverses a broad canvass of human rights issues: freedom from torture, the right to vote, social and economic rights among them.

The exploration of torture is uncomfortable. The rejection of torture as an instrument of military policy by the ANC, is the central fact. The question the narrative suggests is the following. How could advanced democracies have so compromised themselves as to fall under the sway of torture, when these powerless individuals, who faced the terrifying ideology, power and violence of the apartheid state, rejected it?

When the ANC rejected torture, it was faced with the question which we all ultimately face: *"Who are we?"*

---

[71] Albie Sachs, p 279

This same question faced the perpetrators of human rights violations and ultimately the whole country before the South African Truth and Reconciliation Commission:

> "... Sergeant Benzien [was asked to show] the Commission how he had put wet canvas bags over the heads of prisoners. 'Show the Commission how you would smother us until we thought we were drowning, that we would suffocate and die.' ... 'Can you explain how one human being can do this to another human being?' The sergeant started crying. ... because he had been asked a simple question: **How can one person do this to another person?** ... It was asked with a sense of amazement, of horror. What was at stake was affirmation of the values of our society ... It was a question of what kind of people we were. What were we about? What kind of country did we live in? ... It was the image of the weeping former torturer that became perhaps the most remembered one of the whole truth and reconciliation proceedings."[72]

Bureaucratic authoritarianism had been intrinsic to apartheid; the majority of people simply did not count as human beings, hence the squalid housing and inferior education for the majority.

The struggles of the Court in interpreting the new human rights laden constitution, are no less intriguing than the human stories. The Court explores rights in a variety of

---

[72] Albie Sachs, p 24

dimensions and how it deals with the right to vote and the right to life are both of interest.

In *August v Electoral Commission and Others* (1999) the Court ruled on whether prisoners had the right to vote.

> *"SACHs J: ... The vote of each and every citizen is a badge of dignity and personhood. Quite literally, it says that everybody counts."*[73]

In the *Mohamed Case*, the Court affirmed that everyone has the right to life, even foreigners. The case involved the deportation by South African authorities of an asylum seeker who was wanted in the United States on terrorism charges and ultimately faced the death penalty (a penalty abolished by the Court in 1995).

> *"THE COURT: ... In handing Mohamed over to the United States without securing an assurance that he would not be sentenced to death, the immigration authorities failed to give any value to Mohamed's right to life, his right to have his human dignity respected and protected and his right not to be subjected to cruel, inhuman or degrading punishment ... It is inconsistent with the government's obligation to protection the right to life of everyone in South Africa ..."*[74]

Albie Sachs' life and the eventual liberation of South Africa from the grips of apartheid are entwined. His life

---

[73] Albie Sachs, p 122
[74] Albie Sachs, p 40

spans human rights work, suffering as a victim of human rights violations and finally working as a constitutional judge in breathing life into the new South African constitution (a constitution based on human rights).

For anyone interested in human rights work, *The Strange Alchemy of Law and Life* deserves to be read. For those who recall the fall of apartheid and its replacement by a South Africa committed to racial equality and human rights – the transformation and how it was implemented are nothing short of a miracle. His book reminds us that no matter how real the miracle, its agents were ordinary human beings who worked and, in many cases, suffered for their cause.

CHAPTER ELEVEN
Epilogue

The stories we have read are painfully few and many names, well-known and not, have not appeared here. A focus on individual lives of course helps as a storytelling device. It helps us to *"walk in another shoes"*. Yet it also distorts, for individuals do not exist in isolation. Around them are families and communities which have made their lives possible and who have walked alongside them on their journeys, even though we may not see them. The figures we have explored must therefore stand for much more than just themselves. They stand for everyone who walked alongside them, and everyone who helped them on their journey.

So many more stories could be told, and you may wish to seek them out for yourself. Paul Gordon Lauren's *Evolution of Human Rights - Visions Seen,* is a good place to start. It is an extensive account of numerous human rights struggles that span the planet and human history. Lauren is particularly concerned with introducing us to the people who were involved; and he weaves an account rich in detail. Mary Ann Glendon's *A World Made New* beautifully narrates the story of the creation of the Universal Declaration of Human Rights.

In the bibliography, you will find other works listed, including the original works and words of some of those whose stories have been told.

There are many other works and sources. It is particularly important to note that virtually every country has its own figures who are like those we have described here. Those who fought for indigenous rights, or the rights of workers, who sought or extended protection to those fleeing persecution, or those facing discrimination because of their beliefs, their politics, identity or physical characteristics. Most of them are unsung. Among the lesser known are scientists who, pursuing their calling, demolished "scientific racism". Among them are journalists who are targeted for bringing truth to their readers.

Eleanor Roosevelt said that human rights are only real if they find expression close to home: in places so small they are not marked on a map. Perhaps in the lives we have explored we see that human rights are even more intimate than that. Human rights only become real in the human heart. That is their home. They are, most deeply, an active and transformative spark which human beings have discovered in themselves and each other in every generation: a spark that teaches us what human dignity means and how to walk in its path.

Bibliography

Abdu'l Baha, **Memorials of the Faithful**, Baha'i eBooks Publications eBook version 1.10

Sabir Afaqi and Jan T. Jasion (editors), **Tahirih in History: Perspectives on Qurratu'l Ayn from East and West**, Kalimat Press Los Angeles, 2004

Edwin Black, **War Against the Weak Eugenics and America's Campaign to Create a Master Race,** New York 2003

Christopher Buck, **Alain Locke – Faith and Philosophy**, Kalimat Press, Los Angeles, 2005

Christopher Buck and Betty Fisher, **Four Talks Redefining Democracy, Education and World Citizenship**, World Order, Vol 38, No 3

Paolo G. Carozza, **From Conquest to Constitutions: Retrieving a Latin American Tradition of the Idea of Human Rights**, Human Rights Quarterly 25 (2003) 281–313

Thomas Clarkson, **The History of the Rise, Progress, and Accomplishment of the Abolition of the Slave-Trade, but the British Parliament,** 1839 https://www.gutenberg.org/files/10633/10633-h/10633-h.htm

Lawrence Clayton, **Bartolome de las Casas and the African Slave Trade**, History Compass 7/6 (2009): 1526–

1541

Frederick Douglass (1), **The Essential Writings**, Createspace North Charleston, SC, 2013

Frederick Douglass (2). **In the Words of Frederick Douglass: Quotations from Liberty's Champion**, edited by John R. McKivigan, and Heather L. Kaufman, Cornell University Press, 2013.

Frederick Douglass (3), **The Life and Times of Frederick Douglass**, revised edition, Boston 1892

Shoghi Effendi, **God Passes By**, Baha'i Publishing Trust, Wilmette 1944,1974

Henry Epps, **A Concise Chronicle History of the African-American people Experience in America: From Slavery to the White House!**

Susan Gammage, **A Gathering of the Poems of Tahirih**, http://www.ninestarsolutions.com/a-gathering-of-the-poems-of-tahirih

Mahatma Gandhi, Letter to the Director General of UNESCO, 25 May 1947, **UNESCO Human Rights Comments and Interpretation - A Symposium Edited by UNESCO** PHS/3(rev.) https://unesdoc.unesco.org/ark:/48223/pf0000155042

Paul Gilroy. **Race and the Right to be Human.** 2009 Inaugural Address University of Utrecht, Treaty of Utrecht Chair.

Mary Ann Glendon. **A World Made New – Eleanor Roosevelt and the Universal Declaration of Human**

Rights, Random House, 2002

Leonard Harris (ed), **The Philosophy of Alain Locke – Harlem Renaissance and Beyond**, Temple University Press Philadelphia, 1989

Ivo Herzer (ed), **The Italian Refuge - Rescue of the Jews During the Holocaust**, 1989

In Your Hands A Guide for Community Action 1958 https://www.carnegiecouncil.org/publications/100_for_100/in-your-hands-a-guide-for-community-action/_res/id=Attachments/index=0/InYourHandsEdit%20(2).pdf

Zaid Jilani, **What the "Santa Clausification" of Martin Luther King Jr. Leaves Out** https://theintercept.com/2017/01/16/what-the-santa-clausification-of-martin-luther-king-jr-leaves-out/

Martin Luther King Jr., **Loving Your Enemies**, Dexter Avenue Baptist Church, 17 November 1957 https://kinginstitute.stanford.edu/king-papers/documents/loving-your-enemies-sermon-delivered-dexter-avenue-baptist-church

Martin Luther King Jr., **My Trip to the Land of Gandhi**, 1959, https://kinginstitute.stanford.edu/king-papers/documents/my-trip-land-gandhi

Martin Luther King Jr., **Letter from a Birmingham Jail**, 16 April 1963 https://kinginstitute.stanford.edu/encyclopedia/letter-birmingham-jail

Martin Luther King Jr., **Acceptance Speech, The Nobel**

Peace Prize, 10 December 1964 https://www.nobelprize.org/prizes/peace/1964/king/26142-martin-luther-king-jr-acceptance-speech-1964/

Martin Luther King Jr., **The American Dream (1964)**, Drew University, Madison New Jersey, https://depts.drew.edu/lib/archives/online_exhibits/king/speech/theamericandream.pdf

Martin Luther King Jr., **The American Dream (1965)**, Ebenezer Baptist Church, Atlanta, Georgia, 4 July 1965 https://kinginstitute.stanford.edu/king-papers/publications/knock-midnight-inspiration-great-sermons-reverend-martin-luther-king-jr-4

Martin Luther King Jr., **Independence Day Speech** (transcript), "The American Dream", 4 July 1965 https://www.rev.com/blog/transcripts/the-american-dream-july-4th-speech-transcript-martin-luther-king-jr

Martin Luther King Jr., **Transcript of Speech at Southern Methodist University** (SMU) 17 March 1966 https://www.smu.edu/News/2014/mlk-at-smu-transcript-17march1966

Martin Luther King Jr., **Beyond Vietnam**, 4 April 1967 https://kinginstitute.stanford.edu/king-papers/documents/beyond-vietnam

Martin Luther King Jr., **I've Been to the Mountaintop**, 3 April 1968 https://kinginstitute.stanford.edu/encyclopedia/ive-been-mountaintop

Shira Klein, **Italy's Jews From Emancipation to Racism**,

Cambridge University Press, 2018

Nick Kotz, **Judgement Days: Lyndon Baines Johnson, Martin Luther King Jr., and the Laws that Changed America**, Houghton Mifflin 2005

Primo Levi, **The Periodic Table**, Shocken Books, 1995

Alain Locke (ed), **The New Negro: Voices of the Harlem Renaissance**, Touchstone, 1925

Charles Malik, **Representative of Lebanon and Chairman of the Third Committee of the United Nations, Statement** on 6 November 1948 http://webtv.un.org/watch/universal-declaration-of-human-rights-statement-by-mr.-charles-malik/2804615246001

Francis Augustus MacNutt, **Bartholomew de Las Casas; his life, apostolate, and writings,** Cleveland, U.S.A. The Arthur H. Clark Company 1909

Charles Molesworth (ed), **The Works of Alain Locke**, Oxford University Press, 2012

National Public Radio, **The Story of King's "Beyond Vietnam"** 30 March 2010

George Sanderlin (ed., trans.), Bartolome de Las Casas: **Witness: Writings of Bartolome de Las Casas.** (Maryknoll: Orbis books, 1993) 66-67

Martha L. Root, **Tahirih the Pure**, Kalimat Press Los Angeles 1938, 2000

The Schomberg Centre for Research in Black Culture, The New York Public Library, Free Press 2003

James Q. Whitman, **Hitler's American Model: The United States and the Making of Nazi Race Law**. Princeton University Press 2017

Jean Fagan Yellin and John C. Van Horne (eds.), **The Abolitionist Sisterhood: Women's Political Culture in Antebellum America**, Cornell University Press 1994

Joshua D. Zimmerman (ed), **Jews in Italy under Fascist and Nazi Rule 1922-1945**, Cambridge University Press 2005

About the Author

Michael Curtotti is an online writer and has published over 350 articles at his website titled Beyond Foreignness (https://beyondforeignness.org). Michael is a member of the Human Rights Council of Australia Inc. In the late 1990s and early 2000s, he worked in the human rights sector while working for the Australian Baha'i Community. During that time, he served as Secretary of the Australian Forum of Human Rights Organisations and represented Australian NGOs at the UN Commission on Human Rights. He is a practising lawyer, working for the ANUSA Legal Service, which provides pro bono legal services to university students. He is a writer and translator in his spare time. Michael holds a Master of International Law and a PhD in Computer Science. He has contributed as an Honorary Lecturer in the ANU Research School of Computer Science. He has supervised students for the project Information Technology and the Propagation of Racism in the Australian Community. Michael was born in Italy and grew up in Australia. He is married and has three children.

Michael Curtotti

By the Same Writer

Italian Stories

The Dragon the Witch and the Daughters (Il Drago) by Luigi Capuano (English Edition), translated by Michael Curtotti

Matteo Bandello, Romeo and Juliet A New English Translation by Michael Curtotti

Matteo Bandello, Romeo and Juliet A New English Translation by Michael Curtotti, English-Italian Parallel Edition

200 Articles in 200 Days

The Abolition of Foreignness

The Welcome in Nancy Jin & Rosalind Moran (eds.) *These Strange Outcrops: Writing and Art from Canberra*

Michael Curtotti

www.ingramcontent.com/pod-product-compliance
Lightning Source LLC
Chambersburg PA
CBHW072336300426
44109CB00042B/1644